THE
GIFT
OF THE
GREEK

THE
GIFT
OF THE
GREEK

75 Authentic Recipes for the Mediterranean Diet

Yiota Giannakopoulou

Skyhorse Publishing

Skyhorse Publishing books may be purchased in bulk at special discounts for sales promotion, corporate gifts, fund-raising, or educational purposes. Special editions can also be created to specifications. For details, contact the Special Sales Department, Skyhorse Publishing, 307 West 36th Street, 11th Floor, New York, NY 10018 or info@skyhorsepublishing.com.

Skyhorse® and Skyhorse Publishing® are registered trademarks of Skyhorse Publishing, Inc.®, a Delaware corporation.

Visit our website at www.skyhorsepublishing.com.

10 9 8 7 6 5 4 3 2 1

Library of Congress Cataloging-in-Publication Data is available on file.

Cover design by Jane Sheppard

Print ISBN: 978-1-5107-2557-7

Ebook ISBN: 978-1-5107-2558-4

Printed in China

DEDICATIONS

I dedicate this book to Maria Michael-Giannakopoulou, the kindest nurse matron the General Hospital of Nafplio has ever seen, and my mother. Also, with love to my Paul and to our Hugo, Sheldon, Beatrice, and Rincewind.

TABLE OF CONTENTS

INTRODUCTION   1

APPETIZERS AND SALADS   **5**
Vine Leaf and Rice Rolls (Ντολμαδάκια Γιαλαντζί)   6
Butter Beans (Γίγαντες Γιαχνί)   8
Traditional Lettuce Salad with a Vinaigrette Sauce (Μαρουλοσαλάτα)   10
Peasants' Salad (Χωριάτικη Σαλάτα)   12
Honey and Sesame Cheese (Σαγανάκι)   14
Seafood Salad (Σαλάτα με Θαλασσινά)   16
Swirly Cheese Pie (Στριφτή Τυρόπιτα)   18
Shrimp in a Tomato and Ouzo Sauce (Γαρίδες Σαγανάκι)   20
Bulgur Wheat and Feta Cheese Salad (Σαλάτα με Πλιγούρι και Τυρί Φέτα)   22
Puy Lentil, Tuna, and Rice Salad (Σαλάτα με Φακές, Τόνο και Ρύζι.)   24
Potato Salad with Greek Yogurt (Πατατοσαλάτα με Στραγγιστό Γιαούρτι)   26

MAIN DISHES   **29**
Garden Peas with Carrots and Potatoes (Αρακάς)   30
Chickpea Soup (Ρεβυθόσουπα)   32
Spinach and Feta Cheese Pie (Σπανακόπιτα)   34
Stuffed Squid (Γεμιστά Καλαμαράκια)   37
Quick and Easy Leftover Pork and Orzo Pasta Stew   40
Cauliflower and Rice (Κουνουπίδι με Ρύζι)   42
Puy Lentil Stew (Φακές)   44
Quick and Easy Green Beans (Φασολάκια)   46
Bean Broth (Φασολάδα)   48
Mum's Chicken and Rice Soup with a Lemon and Egg Sauce
  (Κοτόσουπα Αυγολέμονο)   50
Smyrna Meatballs (Σουτζουκάκια Σμυρνέικα)   52
Lemon Chicken with Rice (Κοτόπουλο Λεμονάτο)   54
Mince Pie (Κιμαδόπιτα)   56
Chicken Giouvetsi (Κοτόπουλο Γιουβέτσι)   58
Yiota's Chicken Kebab (Γύρος Κοτόπουλο)   60

Family Pork Roast (Χοιρινό στη Γάστρα) 62

Steamed Mussels (Μύδια Αχνιστά) 64

Mama Vivi's Haddock with Leeks (Μπακαλιάρος με Πράσο της Μαμάς Βιβής) 66

Trout Fillet with Spinach (Γοφάρι με Σπανάκι) 68

Sea Bream with Vegetables and Potatoes (Φαγκρί με Λαχανικά και Πατάτες) 70

Moussaka (Μουσακάς) 72

Pasta Pie (Παστίτσιο) 76

Chicken Breast with Mediterranean Roasted Vegetables (Μπριάμ με Κοτόπουλο) 78

Halloumi Pita with Salad and Black Forest Ham (Χαλουμόπιτα) 80

Okras Giahni (Μπάμιες) 82

Beef Stifado (Μοσχάρι Στιφάδο) 84

Mum's Stuffed Vegetables (Γεμιστά) 86

Wine and Tomato Chicken with Linguine (Κόκορας Κρασάτος) 88

Linguine with Homemade Pesto (Λινγκουίνι με Σπιτικό Πέστο) 90

DIPS **93**

Tzatziki (Τζατζίκι) 94

Eggplant Dip (Μελιτζανοσαλάτα) 96

Yellow Split Pea Dip (Φάβα) 98

Hummus (Χούμους) 100

Feta Cheese and Sweet Red Pepper Dip (Ντίπ με Φέτα και Κόκκινη Πιπεριά) 102

Sweet Red Pepper Salsa Dip (Σάλσα Κόκκινης Πιπεριάς) 104

Harissa Dip (Ντίπ με Χαρίσα) 106

Sesame Paste (Ταχίνι) 108

Granddad Georgios's Garlic Potatoes (Σκορδαλιά) 110

BREADS **113**

Greek Pita Bread (Πίτα) 114

Halloumi Pie (Χαλλουμωτή) 116

Lagana Bread (Λαγάνα) 118

Black Olive Bread (Ελιόψωμο) 120

Seeded Bread with Sultanas and Raisins
(Πολύσπορο Ψωμί με Μαύρες Σταφίδες και Σουλτανίνες) 122

SWEETS **125**

Cream-filled Filo Pastry Pie (Μπουγάτσα) 126

Hard Christmas Cookies (Κουραμπιέδες)   128

Fried Filo Pastry Bites in Syrup (Κουρκουμπίνια)   130

Greek Doughnuts (Λουκουμάδες)   132

Twice-Baked Greek Style Biscotti (Διπλοφουρνιστά Παξιμάδια)   134

Ravani (Ραβανί)   136

Greek Soft Christmas Honey Cookies (Μελομακάρονα)   138

Auntie Sofia's Sweet Pumpkin Pie (Κολοκυθένια)   140

Greek Churros (Τουλουμπάκια)   142

INDEX   145

CONVERSION CHARTS   155

ACKNOWLEDGMENTS   157

INTRODUCTION

Greek cuisine is one of the healthiest in the world. It is a cornucopia of fresh produce, flavorful herbs, and recipes that have been passed down through generations. In Greece, food is more than sustenance, it is a celebration, an occasion. It's the centerpiece of every holiday and every circumstance—the thing that brings families and friends together, and the passion that we all share.

Food was an intrinsic part of Ancient Greek myth and legend, from the ambrosia eaten by the gods to the magical apples gifted to Hera. It is woven into every facet of Greek history, from the loukoumades gifted to successful Olympians to the sacrifices made to ensure prosperous harvests. And it is the thing that ensures modern Greeks remain connected to their roots and culture, even when everything else seems to be falling apart around them.

The unique ecosystem of the Greek isles means they are home to some of the world's best oils, fruits, and wines, while Greece's role as one of the oldest civilizations means it has influenced many of the recipes common in Italian, Spanish, and Northern European cuisines. In recent years, it has also been pinpointed as one of the healthiest cuisines in the world, which has inspired many to convert to the Greek way of life.

Greece is my home. It is where I was born, raised, and educated, and it was where I learned to cook the dishes you will find in this book. From a very young age I helped my parents and grandparents prepare dishes, for my father's side of the family in Greece, and my mother's side in Cyprus. This is where I learned the basics of Greek, Cypriot, and Mediterranean cuisine, and where I discovered a passion for cooking.

In later years, after I left my home in the small town of Nafplio to attend university in Athens, food became my ticket to independence. My skills in the kitchen meant that I always ate well, even when living in student digs on a strict budget, with nothing but a single pan, a secondhand microwave, and an oven that had a mind of its own.

When I was twenty-three I moved to the United Kingdom and entered a different world, one where processed foods were more common, and where "home-grown" was a marketing gimmick and not the norm. I continued to cook and it continued to play a big role in my life. It even transformed the health of my partner, a UK native who had previously subsisted on a diet of British meals based on butter and pastry, but now lives as a healthy vegetarian enjoying all the benefits of the Greek diet.

Those benefits stem from the fact that Greeks rely on fresh, homegrown produce and on seasonal dishes. My grandfather, Pappou George, was a big proponent of homegrown food. He lived in a small village in the middle of nowhere. He didn't have access to modern conveniences and for the most part he didn't have basic amenities, but he worked hard as a farmer, he ate well, and he was very healthy.

He believed that if you passed gas when planting onion seeds they would grow to be strong . . . crazy belief. But as odd as some of his practices were, he lived a life that let him eat the food he wanted and live off the land, and he ended up living to nearly one hundred years old as a result. That's what healthy food is to me. It's not food made in a factory and designed to be low fat or low sugar. It's not food that begins life in a lab and ends it in a jar or a squeezable bottle. It's food that is always natural, fresh, and straight from the land.

My grandfather didn't quite make it to 100, but he was climbing mountains (to prove that he could) and living life to his very last day. He never lost his mental or physical faculties and he was able to watch his children and grandchildren grow into healthy adults. I firmly believe that all of this was due to the food he ate and the lifestyle he led, and that's what this book is all about.

I have included recipes that Pappou George himself created and passed down, and I have also included recipes from my father, who is currently still going strong as he approaches 70. I have also included quotes from family members who passed on their recipes and their wisdom.

This is modern Greek and Mediterranean cuisine, but with influences from my family and with my own twist added here and there. What makes Greek food so good and so healthy is not a lack of sugar or fat. We use copious amounts of olive oil and we're not afraid to eat big portions. The difference is that Greek cuisine is rich in *healthy* fats and nutritious produce. It is a diet based on the fruits of the land as well as the sea, so it's one that is naturally low in red meats and processed food, and one that is often vegan and vegetarian friendly.

Diet food should be healthy food, not food loaded with fat substitutes and chemical sweetness and then processed to within an inch of its life. It should be natural, fresh. And on occasion, it should also be a little naughty, a little too sweet and a little too fattening, because what's the point of living if you can't indulge every now and then?

That, in essence, is what *The Gift of the Greek* is. If you want to eat well, stay healthy, and live longer, then this is the book and these are the recipes for you. If you want to lose weight on top of that, then just try to eat less of it. If you begin with a solid foundation of fresh produce, scratch-cooking, and exciting recipes, then everything else is down to portion control—which I am not very good at myself, but hey, you only live once! So, let's get down to it!

APPETIZERS AND SALADS

The Greek salad is one of the most popular and instantly recognizable Greek dishes. It's often the first thing that travelers fall in love with and the first thing they try to replicate when they return home. This chunky, flavorful dish is the epitome of Greek cuisine. It focuses on simple ingredients that are stripped back to basics, and it's very good for you.

It's the dish you'll get if you order a Greek salad in a US/UK-based Greek restaurant, but there are many more variations prepared in homes, delis, and cafes throughout the Greek isles. These dishes are great as light lunches and brunches, or as an appetizer for a bigger family meal.

Some are healthier than others, some are fresher than others, but they all focus on big flavors, quality ingredients, and, for the most part, simple cooking. That's not necessarily true for all Greek dishes and it's certainly not true for many of the main meals in this book. But we're starting with the fundamentals to give you a taste of Mediterranean cooking at its basic best.

Papa Tasso on melitzanosalata: «Δώσε μου μελιτζανοσαλάτα και είμαι χαρούμενος!»

Translation: "Give me some bread and melitzanosalata and I'll be happy forever."

VINE LEAF AND RICE ROLLS
(Ντολμαδάκια Γιαλαντζί)

Serves 15

There are several different kinds of dolma, which literally means "wrapped." Traditionally, dolmadakia (pronounced doma-tha-kia) are made using a combination of rice and minced pork or beef. This dish can be found in Turkey, Greece, and Middle Eastern countries, like Iran. This recipe will only use rice, as I believe this dish is tasty enough without meat. However, adding meat is delicious and simple enough for the carnivores among us as well!

Ingredients

30 vine leaves (sold preserved in brine)

1 cup extra-virgin olive oil

1 red onion (finely chopped)

½ cup pine nuts

½ cup raisins

1½ cups Arborio rice

7 cups boiling water, divided

6 green onions (sliced)

1 bunch fresh dill (finely chopped)

3 mint leaves

Juice of 1 lemon

Salt and freshly ground pepper to taste

Method

1. Remove the vine leaves from the jar, place them on a sieve and wash them thoroughly, using cold water. Make sure they are relatively dry before using them.

2. Heat ½ cup of extra-virgin olive oil in a large frying pan and sauté the onions, until they become transparent.

3. Add the pine nuts and raisins to the pan.

Tip:

Eat hot or cold. Serve with tzatziki dip or with a dollop of plain yogurt. Enjoy!

4. Add the rice and stir, before adding 1 cup of boiling water and boiling for approximately 5 minutes. Remove from the heat and leave to stand for approximately 10 minutes.

5. Add the green onions, dill, and mint in a large bowl and add the rice mixture to it. Season and stir thoroughly.

6. Place a vine leaf flat on a wooden chopping board, shiny side down. Get one teaspoon of the mixture and place it in the middle of the vine leaf. Fold the sides inwards and roll. Repeat the process until you have no mixture, or no vine leaves left. Make sure you keep 3 of the vine leaves to layer the bottom of the pan with.

7. Layer the bottom of a large frying pan with the remaining vine leaves and place the rolls in a circular shape, one next to the other. Once you have no space left, start layering a new layer on the top of the existing one.

8. Pour the rest of the oil, the lemon juice, and 6 cups of boiling water over the rolls. Ensure the liquid covers all the rolls.

9. This is the interesting part. Place a lid or large plate upside down on the rolls and bring to a boil with it still on them. This will ensure the rolls do not split open.

10. Cook on medium heat for approximately 40 minutes. Once the vine leaves become soft and the rice is cooked, remove from the fire and leave to rest for 10 minutes.

BUTTER BEANS
(Γίγαντες Γιαχνί)

Serves 4

The gigantes giaxni (pronounced gi-ga-ntes gia-hnee) is a cheap, cheerful, and easy-to-make dish that is packed with the nutritious value of beans. So, let's get down to it!

Ingredients

400 g. canned butter beans
  (or 2 cups dry beans)
½ cup olive oil
2 red onions (finely chopped)
2 garlic cloves (finely chopped)
½ tsp. chili flakes
1 can chopped tomatoes

½ Tbsp. granulated sugar
Salt and freshly ground black
  pepper to taste
Fresh flat leaf parsley (roughly
  chopped)

Method

1. (Skip this step if you are using canned butter beans.) Soak the beans in some water for at least 7 hours. Once they are puffed up, you can start preparing the sauce.
2. Heat some olive oil in a medium pan and add the onions, garlic, and chili flakes.
3. Add the chopped tomatoes and sugar, and stir well.
4. Add salt and freshly ground black pepper to taste.
5. Replace the lid and leave to simmer for 15 minutes.
6. In a separate sauce pan, put the soaked beans in water, enough to cover the beans entirely. Boil for approximately 40 minutes, until soft.

7. Take the pan off the heat, and drain the beans' water into a bowl. Keep for later. Return the beans to the pan and mix with the sauce. Use a bit of the water you boiled the beans in, and simmer for approximately 15 minutes. Use more of the boiled water, as required.

8. Serve on a plate, drizzle with extra-virgin olive oil, and sprinkle the parsley. Season to taste and enjoy!

TRADITIONAL LETTUCE SALAD WITH A VINAIGRETTE SAUCE
(Μαρουλοσαλάτα)

I will never forget the look on my British in-laws' faces when my father walked in the house while we were on holiday in Greece, with an average (to him) sized head of lettuce. They turned around and said "Oh dear Lord, what on earth is that?" You see, vegetables really do love the sun, and given the fact that the UK does not enjoy much, produce of that caliber rarely appear in our markets. The Greek maroulosalata (pronounced ma-roo-lo-sa-la-ta) is a staple of the Greek diet, accompanying a plethora of dishes, from meat to fish and vegetables.

Ingredients

1 head romaine lettuce

1 red onion

1 cup feta cheese (cubed)

Kalamata olives (as many as your
   heart desires)

½ bunch flat leaf parsley (coarsely
   chopped)

1 cucumber, sliced

For the sauce

4 Tbsp. extra-virgin olive oil

7 Tbsp. Dijon mustard

2 Tbsp. honey

8 Tbsp. balsamic vinegar

Salt and pepper to taste

Tip:
Add croutons, tomatoes, and capers for a more distinctive taste.

Method

1. Wash the lettuce thoroughly and chop it roughly.
2. Slice the onion into rings and add to the lettuce.
3. Add the feta cheese and the Kalamata olives.
4. Add the chopped flat leaf parsley and the cucumber.

For the sauce

1. Pour the olive oil, mustard, honey, and balsamic vinegar into a mixing bowl and mix thoroughly. Add salt and pepper.
2. Pour over your salad and enjoy!

PEASANTS' SALAD
(Χωριάτικη Σαλάτα)

Serves 4

Summers in Greece are hot—common knowledge, I know—but sometimes you just don't feel like eating a main meal, especially after you return from a five-hour trip to the beach. One of the most popular food choices for too-hot-to-eat days has always been the horiatiki salata (pronounced cho-ree-a-tee-kee) with its refreshing combination of fresh and flavorsome ingredients. The most important thing is to ensure that the oil you use is of exceptional quality, otherwise this little culinary gem can lose its appeal. The tomato was introduced to Greece in 1818, but it was not an immediate success. When the tomato was finally integrated into Greek cuisine, it had many uses; however, not many of them included using the tomato as an ingredient for salads. This "peasants' salad" is a relatively new addition to Greece's rich cuisine. I suspect that the name originates from farmers who used to take each of these ingredients, along with some homemade bread, and pack them whole in the little bundle they carried on their shoulders, much like we do today in our plastic sandwich packs.

Ingredients

3 ripe tomatoes

½ cucumber

1 red onion

⅓ cup extra-virgin olive oil

½ cup Kalamata olives

1½ cups feta cheese (crumbled)

Generous pinch of dried oregano

Salt and pepper, to taste

Method

1. Slice the tomatoes into eighths.
2. Thinly slice the cucumbers and red onion.
3. Combine all the ingredients in a deep bowl.
4. Add the oil, Kalamata olives, and the crumbled feta cheese, and sprinkle the oregano.
5. Season with salt and pepper to taste.

HONEY AND SESAME CHEESE
(Σαγανάκι)

Serves 4

A staple starter in every Greek food gathering, the saganaki (pronounced sa-ga-na-kee) is a dish that everyone wants a piece of. It is to be treated as a meze, as one cannot consume a lot of it; it is quite filling and rich.

Ingredients

2 Tbsp. all-purpose flour

1 tsp. sugar

3 Tbsp. olive oil

120 g. saganaki cheese (gouda will do)

Bowl of cold water

1 Tbsp. honey

1 Tbsp. toasted sesame seeds

Method

1. Mix the flour and the sugar.
2. Heat some olive oil into a shallow frying pan.
3. Quickly dip the cheese in the flour mixture, then dip in some cold water and into the flour mixture again. Then quickly put the cheese into the pan. Be careful; the oil might spit when the cheese hits the hot surface.
4. Once the cheese turns a nice golden brown color, remove from the heat and rest on some paper towels.
5. Drizzle with some honey and sprinkle with toasted sesame seeds.

SEAFOOD SALAD
(Σαλάτα με Θαλασσινά)

Serves 2

There are seafood taverns all over Greece, and the aroma they emit is very inviting. You can choose your fish and seafood just after they are caught. Given the fact that not everyone has that same access to fresh seafood, however, one might have to be creative for this recipe!

Ingredients

Any mix of salad leaves:

Red butterhead lettuce

Rocket

Red chard

Mizuna

Red batavia

Baby spinach

½ lb. octopus (in brine)

½ lb. squid (in brine)

⅓ lb. mussels (in brine)

1 tsp. pomegranate molasses

1 Tbsp. balsamic vinegar

1 Tbsp. extra-virgin olive oil

Salt and pepper to taste

Method

1. Place the salad leaves on a plate.
2. Drain then scatter the seafood bits around the plate.
3. Drizzle with the pomegranate molasses, vinegar, and olive oil, mixed together or drizzled individually.
4. Salt and pepper to taste.

SWIRLY CHEESE PIE
(Στριφτή Τυρόπιτα)

Serves 6

A firm favorite for any kind of celebration buffet, the tiropita (pronounced tee-ro-pee-ta) is always one of the first things to disappear before your eyes. There are many ways to prepare tiropita, but one of the more traditional forms is that of a swirl. It can be served as it is, or it can be cut into individual pieces for a finger buffet.

Ingredients

4 eggs

1 cup Greek yogurt (full fat)

2½ cups feta cheese (crumbled)

1 cup ricotta cheese

Salt and pepper to taste

1 pack filo pastry sheets

5 Tbsp. melted butter

Method

1. Preheat the oven to 350°F.
2. Beat the eggs and fold in the yogurt and the cheeses. If you have time to blend the cheeses using a hand blender, it will help your tiropita swirl look even with no lumps and bumps.
3. Season to taste with the salt and pepper.
4. This is the tricky part. Take one pastry sheet and lay it on your working surface. Brush with some butter, attach another filo sheet approximately two inches before the previous sheet ends, on the short edge. Repeat the process, until all filo sheets are used.

5. Put the filling in a straight line along the length of your filo pastry sheets. Start folding upwards in a roll carefully, until you have a long, thin, sausage-like structure. Start forming a swirl, like a snail's shell, starting from the inside swirl and wrapping around until closed.

6. Brush with butter. Bake on a flat oven tray for approximately 40 minutes, or until golden brown.

SHRIMP IN A TOMATO AND OUZO SAUCE
(Γαρίδες Σαγανάκι)

If anyone ever needed the perfect excuse to consume some ouzo, they can make this fantastic dish. Everyone loves shrimp, especially in Greece, in any form, with sauce or without, just fried, on a salad, you name it! Enjoy with freshly made bread and some ouzo, of course! Opa!

Ingredients

1 large red onion

3 garlic cloves

1 medium-sized leek

1 carrot

1 cup extra-virgin olive oil

30 medium shrimps (frozen or fresh)

5 ripe tomatoes (thickly sliced)

1 tsp. fennel seeds

1 shot glass of ouzo

½ cup tomato puree

1½ cups feta cheese (chopped roughly)

1 lemon

3 Tbsp. flat leaf parsley (roughly chopped)

2 Tbsp. freshly chopped dill

Salt and pepper to taste

Method

1. Finely chop the onion, garlic, leek, and carrot, using a food processor.
2. Pour half of the olive oil in a large pan and sauté the shrimps until thoroughly cooked, for approximately 2 to 3 minutes.
3. As soon as the shrimps are a nice golden color, add the vegetable mixture and leave to boil for 2 minutes.
4. Add the tomatoes, fennel seeds, ouzo, and tomato puree to the pan. Pour in the remaining half of the olive oil.

5. Cover the pan and boil on low heat for 10-15 minutes.

6. Preheat the oven to 350°F.

7. Once cooked, place all the ingredients in an oven-safe dish and add the feta cubes on the top.

8. Put the dish in the oven and bake until the feta partially melts and takes a nice color; this should take about 10 minutes.

9. Take the pan off the heat, squeeze a lemon over the saganaki, and serve with chopped flat leaf parsley and freshly chopped dill. Add salt and pepper to taste.

BULGUR WHEAT AND FETA CHEESE SALAD
(Σαλάτα με Πλιγούρι και Τυρί Φέτα)

Ingredients

7 Tbsp. extra-virgin olive oil, divided

1 cup bulgur wheat

1 Tbsp. butter

1 cup water

1 vegetable (or chicken) stock cube

½ cup boiled chestnuts

3 Tbsp. pine nuts

2 scallions

1 garlic clove

1 Tbsp. fresh flat leaf parsley (finely chopped)

2 Tbsp. fresh mint (finely chopped)

1 tsp. oregano

1 lemon (juice and zest)

1 pomegranate

½ cup feta cheese

Salt and pepper to taste

Method

1. Place a frying pan on high heat and pour 3 tablespoons of oil.
2. Add the bulgur wheat and sauté for approximately 5 minutes, or until the wheat takes a golden-brown color. Keep stirring.
3. Add the knob of butter and stir until melted.
4. Pour the water over the wheat and boil until all the water is absorbed.
5. Add the stock cube.
6. Take the pan off the fire, and add the chestnuts and pine nuts. Return to the fire for approximately 5 minutes.
7. Chop the scallions, garlic, parsley, mint, and oregano and mix together.
8. Pour the wheat mixture in a large bowl and add the scallion mixture.
9. Add the remaining 4 tablespoons olive oil, lemon juice, and rind.

10. De-seed the pomegranate and add seeds to the bowl.

11. Crumble the feta cheese on top.

12. Salt and pepper to taste and enjoy!

PUY LENTIL, TUNA, AND RICE SALAD
(Σαλάτα με Φακές, Τόνο και Ρύζι)

Ingredients

1 cup puy lentils

1 cup long grain rice

1 red onion

2 cloves of garlic

½ cup flat leaf parsley

1 Tbsp. fresh mint

¼ cup black olives (pitted and sliced)

3 Tbsp. tahini paste

1 lime (juice and zest)

1 can of tuna (drained)

Salt and pepper to taste

2 Tbsp. extra-virgin olive oil

Method

1. Boil the puy lentils for approximately 25 minutes.
2. In another large saucepan, boil the long grain rice in a large saucepan for approximately 15 minutes.
3. Chop the onion, garlic, flat leaf parsley, and mint.
4. Mix the long grain rice and the lentils. Add the onion, garlic, parsley, mint, and black olives.
5. Pour the tahini paste, lime juice, and zest.
6. Drain the tuna and add to the salad.
7. Salt and pepper to taste.
8. Drizzle the olive oil and enjoy!

POTATO SALAD WITH GREEK YOGURT
(Πατατοσαλάτα με Στραγγιστό Γιαούρτι)

Ingredients

6 large potatoes

1 garlic clove

4 Tbsp. Greek yogurt

1 tsp. paprika

1 tsp. oregano

1 lime (juice and zest)

2 Tbsp. extra-virgin olive oil

½ red onion

2 scallions

1 bunch flat leaf parsley

Salt and pepper to taste

Method

1. Bring a large pot of water to a boil with a pinch of salt.
2. Cut the potatoes into large pieces and add to the pan; cook until soft.
3. Finely chop the garlic clove and add to the Greek yogurt. Add the paprika, oregano, lime juice, zest, and olive oil, and mix well.
4. When the potatoes are soft enough, use a colander to drain the excess water.
5. In a large bowl, mix the potatoes with the yogurt sauce and rough them up with a fork.
6. Finely chop the onion, scallions, and parsley and add to the salad.
7. Add salt and pepper to taste. Serve warm or chilled, according to your preference.

MAIN DISHES

One of the surprising things about Greek cuisine is that it is predominantly vegetarian. You will notice that a lot of the dishes in this book and in this section don't have any meat or fish. That's not by design, it's just that many Greek dishes began as "peasant dishes" and because meat was expensive, it often wasn't included.

Greek cuisine also uses olive oil when other Europe cuisines might use butter or animal shortening, so many of these dishes are also vegan.

There is a ready supply of olive oil in most Greek homes. It's cheap, and in most cases it is produced in olive groves just a few miles away. Many families, mine included, own small plots of olive trees. Every year the owners congregate for the harvest, collecting and then pressing vast amounts of oil, before handing each owner their fair share. At any given time, my father has several two-liter bottles filled to the brim with the finest oil, and even though this same oil would be stuck with a "premium" label and be sold for in excess of $100 a bottle in the US, he pays with a few hours of his time and a dozen empty soda bottles.

So, always invest a little more in a high quality olive oil if you can and resist the temptation to swap it with animal fats and other unhealthy fats. Whether you're vegan or not, it is always better to use olive oil.

As for the type, I personally think Greek oil is the best, but you can also get great oils from Italy and Spain. Taste-wise, it makes a massive difference, but with regards to health, you will get just as many benefits from a cheaper, lower quality oil.

Aunt Sophia on onions and oil: «Όλα τα φαγητά είναι πιο νόστιμα με λίγο κρεμμυδάκι και μπόλικο λαδάκι»

Translation: "Pitas, soups, dips—everything is better with a little red onion and a lot of olive oil."

GARDEN PEAS WITH CARROTS AND POTATOES
(Αρακάς)

Serves 4-5

Arakas (pronounced a-ra-kas). This deliciously sweet vegetable dish is very nutritious and rich in folic acid and Vitamin A. It's also rich in phytonutrients, minerals, vitamins, and antioxidants. The main reason it's part of my household's diet, however, is the fact that it's sweet and filling. Cooked in great quality olive oil definitely makes a difference to this dish, as it is a main meal. Peas for a main meal? Don't judge until you try it!

Ingredients

1 cup olive oil

1 red onion (finely chopped)

4-5 green onions (finely chopped)

2 potatoes cut into cubes

2 sliced carrots

1 Tbsp. tomato puree

1 tsp. granulated sugar

18 oz. frozen garden peas

Salt and freshly ground black pepper

Fresh dill to taste (finely chopped)

Method

1. Heat half the olive oil in a pan and lightly sauté the red onion and green onions. Make sure that at this stage they do not get a lot of color. This should take approximately 3–4 minutes on medium heat.

2. Add the potatoes, carrots, tomato puree, sugar, and peas. Add salt and pepper to taste. Cover the ingredients with approximately 4 cups of water, or until they are half submerged.

3. Cover the pan and leave to boil for approximately 20 minutes. Once the water is almost absorbed and the carrots and potatoes have softened, add the other half of the olive oil and the chopped dill. Boil for another 10–15 minutes until the water has been completely absorbed.

CHICKPEA SOUP
(Ρεβυθόσουπα)

Serves 4

The humble chickpea: that round, white, bullet-like superfood. Chickpeas contain soluble fiber, which helps regulate blood sugar, lower LDL cholesterol, relieve IBS symptoms, and provide protection against bowel cancer. Chickpeas also contain calcium, iron, and zinc, which help maintain healthy bones. They come in many forms, and there are a million ways in which they can be cooked. Revythosoupa (pronounced re-vee-tho-soo-pa) is sure to keep you warm on a winter's night.

Ingredients

- 4 cups canned chickpeas, or 2 cups dried
- 2 tsp. baking soda, divided
- 1 cup olive oil
- Enough cold water to cover chickpeas
- 1 large onion (both red and white would work equally well)
- 1 cube vegetable stock
- Juice of 1 lemon
- Salt and pepper to taste
- 1 red onion for garnish (sliced)

Method

1. (Skip this step if you are using canned chickpeas.) Place the dried chickpeas in a deep bowl, add a teaspoon of baking soda, cover with water, and leave overnight. Drain and wrap them in a clean kitchen towel, and add another teaspoon of baking soda. Place the towel on the table and rub the chickpeas gently, using circular movements, until the shells are separated. Unwrap them, place them in a sieve along with the shells, and wash thoroughly.

2. Place the chickpeas in a pan with the oil and the cold water over them. Peel the onion and add it whole to the water. Bring it to boil.

3. Add the stock cube.

4. Boil the chickpeas for about 1 ½ hours, or until they start softening up. Remove the shells that come to the surface, using a slotted spoon. Stir often.

5. When the chickpeas are soft, turn the heat off and cover the pan with a kitchen towel for about 5 minutes. This will prevent the chickpeas from becoming watery.

6. Serve with a drizzle of olive oil, lemon, a sprinkle of salt and pepper, and some sliced red onion as a garnish.

Tip:
Leftovers can be used to make hummus!

SPINACH AND FETA CHEESE PIE
(Σπανακόπιτα)

Serves 12

Everyone remembers the scene from a famous film about a Greek wedding when the yiayia (grandma) enters the scene with the Spanakopita (pronounced spa-na-ko-pee-ta) at hand, in order to convince the admissions officer representing her granddaughter's university of choice to accept her application. Well, that pretty much sums it up, the spanakopita is the king of pies in Greece, and it is respected and consumed by most.

Ingredients

For the pastry

2½ cups hard flour or all-purpose flour

1 Tbsp. granulated sugar

1 teaspoon salt

1 cup olive oil

½ cup white wine vinegar

1 cup water

¾ cup olive oil (for brushing)

Semolina flour (for dusting)

1 egg (for brushing the top of your pie)

For the filling

5 Tbsp. olive oil

1 leek

4 spring onions (coarsely chopped)

1 red onion

Handful of pine nuts

35 oz. baby spinach leaves

½ bunch fresh mint (coarsely chopped)

½ bunch fresh dill (coarsely chopped)

Zest of one lemon

18 oz. feta cheese

10 oz. cream cheese

10 oz. Greek yogurt

Salt and pepper to taste

Knob of butter for greasing the pan

continued

Method

1. Preheat oven to 350°F.
2. Place the dry ingredients for the filo pastry in a mixer with a dough hook, mix until combined.
3. Add the liquid ingredients, mix until thoroughly combined.
4. Transfer to the working surface and divide into 7 equal parts.
5. Sprinkle some semolina on to the working surface and start to roll out the first of the 7 pieces of dough. Ensure that it is as thin as possible. The semolina flour will ensure the dough is not sticky.
6. Roll out the remaining dough. Set the first rolled-out piece aside, and roll the remaining filo pastry dough sheets. Cut the sheets in half.

For the filling

1. Sauté the leek.
2. Mix all the ingredients together, until unified.

Assembling

1. Grease a round baking pan with some butter. Place 4 pieces of filo pastry in the bottom of the pan. Layer the filo pastry until you cannot see any spots that remain uncovered.
2. Drizzle with olive oil.
3. Add the filling and spread it evenly across the base of your pan.
4. Cover the filling with the remaining filo pastry. Use whole piece of pastry you had set aside to cover the very top of the pie.
5. Beat the egg. Score the surface with a sharp knife and brush with the beaten egg.
6. Bake for an hour, regularly checking your pie until it takes a golden color.

Tip:
It tastes even better the day after, when you eat it cold!

STUFFED SQUID
(Γεμιστά Καλαμαράκια)

Serves 4

I know that seafood can be intimidating to the uninitiated. I wish I had a penny for every time I have heard "Oh, no, I don't do squid and octopus . . . They are chewy and disgusting." Well, my answer is "You didn't have them cooked properly." Squid, similarly to other seafood, needs to be cooked for a long time; it needs tender love and care. Surely enough, when I invited the same people to taste seafood the Greek way, they completely changed their minds. So, here we go, one of the most popular Greek recipes involving squid. Prepare to be amazed!

Ingredients

10 small squid (fresh or frozen)

3 green onions (finely sliced)

2 red onions (or shallots, sliced in rings)

3 cloves garlic (finely chopped)

½ bunch fresh flat leaf parsley

½ bunch fresh dill

3 ripe tomatoes (diced)

½ cup Arborio rice

1½ cups olive oil

Toothpicks (I know, bear with me)

1 pinch of sugar

½ cup dry white wine or ouzo

Salt and pepper to taste

1 lemon

Method

1. If you are of a squeamish disposition, ask a local fisherman or supermarket attendant to do this for you, but if you are up for it, follow this step. Wash the squid thoroughly and separate the squid heads from the bodies. Move the heads to a chopping board and chop them finely. Place them in a bowl.

continued

2. Add the green onions, red onions, and garlic.

3. Reserve some of the parsley and the dill, then roughly chop the rest of the herbs and add them to the bowl.

4. Add half the tomatoes to the bowl, along with the Arborio rice.

5. Pour half of the olive oil in the bowl and mix all the ingredients well.

6. Start stuffing the squid, careful not to overstuff. Once stuffed, secure the opening of the squid by weaving a toothpick through the skin. This should ensure your squid stuffing will not escape the casing. Again, I cannot stress enough that you should not overstuff the squids, as if you do, they will burst open during cooking.

7. Once the above step is done, you are likely to have a bit of stuffing left; do not worry as we will use this during the cooking process.

8. Heat the remaining oil in a large pan, and begin to arrange the squid in a circular manner, approaching the middle of your pan; this will help the squid to take a nice golden brown color.

9. Add the remainder of the tomatoes.

10. Sprinkle the sugar and pour the white wine or ouzo in the pan. If you feel there is not enough liquid for the squid and the rice to cook, feel free to add a pint of water in the pan.

11. Salt and pepper to taste.

12. Cover the pan and let them simmer. Sometimes, you will have to add a bit more water during the cooking process if the squid and the rice absorb the liquids before they become tender.

13. When the squid looks cooked and the rice is nice and soft, remove from the stove. There should be very little liquid left at the bottom of the pan; it should look like a nice thick tomato sauce.

14. Place on a plate and sprinkle the fresh herbs we kept back before.

15. Squeeze a fresh lemon over the top, and enjoy!

QUICK AND EASY LEFTOVER PORK AND ORZO PASTA STEW

Serves 2

Leftover dishes are popular worldwide—making the most of your buck is important, and some recipes taste even better the next day! Dishes like the UK's favorite bubble and squeak, a dish made from leftover Sunday dinner of mashed potato, cabbage, carrot, etc., are popular with savvy, creative families. This leftover pork and orzo stew will keep you warm during winter nights, next to the fire. It is a versatile dish, which you can customize easily to create something entirely different. Your imagination is the limit!

Ingredients

1 cup olive oil

1 red onion (finely chopped)

1 clove garlic (finely chopped)

2 cups leftover pork

1 large carrot (cut into small cubes)

Dried oregano (to taste)

1 can chopped tomatoes

1½ cups orzo pasta

2 cups water

1 cube of chicken stock
   (homemade stock even better)

Salt and freshly ground black
   pepper (to taste)

Method

1. Heat the olive oil in a pan and add the onion and garlic. Sauté until golden.

2. Add the leftover pork and the cubed carrot to the pan; cook for 5 minutes. Add the oregano at this point.

3. Add the chopped tomatoes and orzo pasta. Add the water and stock cube. Leave to simmer until the pasta is cooked thoroughly. This will take approximately 15 minutes.

4. Serve with salt and freshly ground black pepper.

CAULIFLOWER AND RICE
(κουνουπίδι με ρύζι)

Serves 4

Cauliflower is a misunderstood vegetable and, as such, it is not on everyone's favorites list, at least not without it being smothered in cheese. Hopefully, if you follow this recipe, you will re-think your relationship with the humble cauliflower. Cauliflower has many nutrients, including Vitamin C, phosphorus, magnesium, potassium, and manganese.

Ingredients

1½ cups olive oil

1 large red onion (finely chopped)

1 whole head cauliflower

1 small glass of wine (white or red)

3 tablespoons tomato puree

Pinch of cinnamon

Pinch of paprika

Salt and pepper to taste

1 cup risotto rice

Method

1. Heat the oil and sauté the finely chopped onion. Separate the cauliflower into florets and add them to the oil.

2. When the cauliflower becomes a light beige shade, pour in the wine.

3. Add the tomato puree, cinnamon, paprika, salt, and pepper. Cook for approximately 10 minutes, or until the cauliflower has cooked thoroughly. Check it often, to avoid overcooking.

4. Add rice and check there is enough liquid in the pan for the rice to cook. If not, add some boiled water.

5. Once the rice is cooked and all the liquid is absorbed, serve with warm bread and feta cheese.

PUY LENTIL STEW
(Φακές)

Serves 4

Growing up, I refused to even set eyes on the lentils my mother lovingly made for me. As far as I was concerned, they were evil little brown dots, waiting to ruin my dinner that day. My mum used to always tell me that they were rich in iron, and I would be weak if I did not eat them. I always thought she was making it up—guess what, she wasn't! Lentils are rich in fiber, protein, minerals, and vitamins; they are also low in calories and contain virtually no fat. Need I say more?

Ingredients

1 onion (sliced)

1 garlic clove (chopped)

1 cup olive oil

1 bay leaf

1 carrot (cubed)

1 potato (cubed)

2 cups puy lentils

1 cube of vegetable stock + 1 pint of boiling water

Salt and pepper to taste

Olive oil (to drizzle)

Red wine vinegar (to drizzle)

Method

1. Sauté the onion and garlic in olive oil in a pan placed on medium heat.
2. Add the bay leaf, the carrot, and the potato, and shallow fry for 4 minutes.
3. Wash the lentils and add them to the pan along with the vegetable stock. Boil for approximately 30 minutes.
4. Once the lentils, the potatoes, and the carrots are cooked, remove the bay leaf and add salt and pepper to taste.
5. Serve with a drizzle of olive oil and vinegar.

Tip:
Serve with some warm bread and feta cheese.

QUICK AND EASY GREEN BEANS
(Φασολάκια)

Serves 4

Ingredients

1½ cups olive oil

1 large red onion (finely chopped)

1 clove garlic (finely chopped)

1 large carrot (cubed)

2 white potatoes (cubed)

1 bunch of flat leaf parsley
(coarsely chopped)

2 Tbsp. tomato puree

1 can chopped tomatoes

1 cube vegetable stock + 2 cups of
boiled water

35 oz. bag of frozen green beans

Method

1. Heat the olive oil and add the onion and garlic, cooking until golden brown.
2. Add the carrot, potatoes, and coarsely chopped parsley. Leave to cook for 5 minutes before adding the tomato puree, the chopped tomatoes, and the vegetable stock cube dissolved in boiling water.
3. Add the green beans and stir thoroughly.
4. Leave to simmer for approximately 25 minutes, until the water is absorbed and you are only left with the olive oil in the pan.

Tip:
Serve with warm bread and feta cheese.

BEAN BROTH
(φασολάδα)

Serves 4

If Armageddon struck and most food sources were nowhere to be seen, fasolada (pronounced fa-so-la-da) would be my dad's one dish to protect. I am not kidding you; if he was told that he could only eat fasolada every day for the rest of his life, he would be on board, no questions asked. He would say, "The bean is the most nutritious food source around; do not underestimate it, young one!" This recipe is an adaptation from the recipe I learned from him. Thanks, Dad!

Ingredients

2 cups dry white haricot beans

1 cup extra-virgin olive oil

1 large onion (finely chopped)

1 clove garlic (finely chopped)

3 carrots (sliced)

2 celery stalks (diced)

2 large potatoes (quartered)

2 Tbsp. tomato puree

1 bunch of flat leaf parsley (finely chopped)

1 vegetable stock cube

¼ cup boiling water

Salt and pepper to taste

1 lemon (juiced)

Method

1. Place beans in a stock pot. Add enough boiling water to cover. Bring the beans to a boil for approximately 40 minutes, or until soft.

2. Heat the olive oil in a large pan and sauté the onion and garlic.

3. Add the carrots, celery, potatoes, and tomato puree.

4. Add the flat leaf parsley and stir the ingredients thoroughly.

5. Dilute the stock cube in some boiling water. Add it to the pan.

6. Add the parboiled beans, but keep a handful aside for later. Add salt and pepper to taste. Cover with boiling water and simmer for approximately 40 minutes until the vegetables are soft.

7. Mash the handful of beans kept back, and add the mash to the boiling mixture.

8. Stir until the broth has thickened. If the broth is still on the thin side, remove some beans, mash them and add them back in—the starch in the beans will help thicken your broth. Squeeze half a lemon over the top and serve.

Tip:
Save some time by replacing the dry beans with tins of ready boiled haricot beans. Serve with feta cheese and Kalamata olives!

MUM'S CHICKEN AND RICE SOUP WITH A LEMON AND EGG SAUCE
(Κοτόσουπα Αυγολέμονο)

Serves 4

Dark winter nights demand a heartwarming chicken soup, as do colds and sniffles. Mum made this luscious chicken soup for me when I was feeling a bit under the weather, or when my stomach was iffy. An old Greek culinary myth says that when the egg and lemon sauce is being mixed, before it is added to the soup, a couple has to kiss in the kitchen, otherwise it goes horribly wrong and the egg splits! Why this is supposed to happen remains a mystery. If the couple kisses, however, the dish's success with regards to taste and healing properties is an absolute given!

Ingredients

2 chicken breasts

1 carrot

1 cup long grain or risotto rice

1 potato (cubed)

½ red bell pepper (cubed)

1 chicken stock cube

Splash of olive oil

Salt and pepper

For the sauce

1 egg + 1 yolk

2 lemons

Method

1. Boil some water in a large pan and add the chicken breasts. Once they are cooked thoroughly, remove from the water and shred, keeping the water boiling. Set the chicken aside for later.

2. Chop the carrot and add it to the water your chicken was boiled in, along with the rice, potato, and red pepper cubes.

3. Add the chicken stock cube and the splash of olive oil to the boil, cooking for approximately 20 minutes.

4. Once the rice and vegetables are cooked thoroughly, add the shredded chicken and boil for another 5 minutes.

5. Using a ladle, remove 1 cup of broth from the boil, and pour it in a deep dish.

For the sauce

1. In a separate dish, beat one whole egg, along with the yolk from a second egg. Beat the mix, and add the juice of two lemons. Once the ingredients look unified, pour the broth you have removed into the mixture, and beat with a fork.

2. Remove the pan from the heat and gradually add the egg mixture, while stirring vigorously, in order to avoid the egg white splitting. Once this process is done, return to the fire for 5 more minutes.

Tip:
Enjoy with plenty of lemon juice and crusty bread! Yummy!

SMYRNA MEATBALLS
(Σουτζουκάκια Σμυρνέικα)

Serves 4

Traditional Greek cooking was influenced heavily by the presence of the Ottoman empire for the better part of 400 years. It was only natural that a degree of assimilation of Eastern influences would take place in the local cuisine. One of those alchemies brought the "soutzoukaki" to us. Literally, the word means "little sausage," which is in reference to its oblong shape. The Greeks removed the sausage skin and freed the soutzoukaki from its intestinal prison. Traditionally, the soutzoukakia are served with mashed potatoes, rice, or, if you are really being naughty, French fries.

Ingredients

For the meatballs

6 cups ground meat (pork and beef)

3 slices of stale bread (soaked in good red wine), torn into pieces

2 eggs

1 bunch flat leaf parsley

1 tsp. red wine vinegar

1 tsp. cumin seeds

3 cloves garlic

1 tsp. sugar

½ tsp. ground cinnamon

Salt and pepper to taste

Splash of olive oil

For the sauce

4 ripe tomatoes, chopped

2 red onions (finely grated)

1 tsp. sugar

Pinch of allspice

1 cup extra-virgin olive oil

½ tsp. cumin

½ cup red wine

Salt and pepper to taste

Method

1. This is a very simple step. In a large mixing bowl, add all the meatball ingredients, except oil, and knead together until unified. Leave the mixture aside for at least an hour, as this helps the ingredients to bond.

2. Shape the mince mixture into little oblongs. Dip your fingers into a cup of red wine to avoid stickiness. Your meatballs love red wine!

3. Heat a splash of olive oil in a pan and lightly fry the meatballs until thoroughly cooked. Remember, minced meat allows bacteria to escape the surface and contaminate more easily. No pink allowed! Don't turn the heat up; the meatballs need gentle treatment.

For the sauce

1. Preheat oven to 350°F. In a deep, cast-iron skillet, combine the sauce ingredients, and bring the mix to a boil on the stove top.

2. Add the meatballs to the sauce and place in oven for approximately 30 minutes. Check often and baste with the sauce regularly. This process will make your meatballs tender and succulent.

LEMON CHICKEN WITH RICE
(Κοτόπουλο Λεμονάτο)

There are very few dishes that make my mouth water, and this one is definitely one of them. My mum used to make it in the casserole with cubed potatoes instead of rice, and it was a meal I looked forward to eating every time. In fact, I used to look forward to school finishing, so I could go home to a lovely cooked lemon chicken. The flavor is tangy, sweet, and wholesome. It definitely makes your mouth water. Slurp!

Ingredients

1 whole fresh chicken (you can also use chicken fillets, drumsticks, or thighs)
Salt and pepper to taste
1 cup olive oil
1 red onion
1 garlic clove, chopped
1½ cups long grain rice

1 bay leaf
Pinch of rosemary
Pinch of oregano
2 lemons (juice and zest)
3 Tbsp. butter
1 cube chicken stock dissolved in 2 cups boiling water

Method

1. Fillet the chicken into portions, season with salt and pepper, and marinate it in half the olive oil (best if you leave it in the fridge for a few hours to absorb the flavor of the oil).
2. Heat the other half of the oil in a deep stock pot and brown the chicken portions.
3. Slice the onion and add it to the stock pot along with the garlic.
4. Once the onions have caramelized, and the chicken portions are golden brown, add the rice, bay leaf, rosemary, oregano, lemon zest, and the butter.

5. Let the mixture come to a gentle simmer.

6. Add the lemon juice.

7. Add the chicken stock.

8. Reduce heat and let simmer, until the rice has absorbed the liquid and the chicken portions are thoroughly cooked.

9. Salt and pepper to taste.

MINCE PIE
(Κιμαδόπιτα)

Serves 12

Firm favorite of mine, the quick, easy, and satisfying mince pie. According to my friend Persephone, the secret of a good kimadopita (pronounced kee-ma-do-pee-ta) is to use plenty of red onion. The quality of mince is also really important and of course, you can definitely guess it by now, the extra-virgin olive oil. This quick, fuss-free recipe will produce approximately 12 pie pieces, making it a really good dish to include in buffets for celebrations, as it is as tasty cold as it is hot.

Ingredients

5 Tbsp. olive oil, divided

1 large red onion (diced)

Pinch of dried rosemary

Pinch of dried oregano

Pinch of dried thyme

2 carrots

1 celery stick

1 Tbsp. granulated sugar

2 cups minced meat (combination of beef and pork)

3 Tbsp. tomato puree

1 chicken stock cube

½ cup boiling water

3 Tbsp. gruyere cheese (finely grated)

1 egg

½ Tbsp. extra-virgin olive oil or butter, for greasing

2 sheets of ready rolled puff pastry (life is too short to make your own puff pastry)

Salt and pepper to taste

Olive oil or butter (for greasing)

Method

1. Preheat the oven to 350°F.
2. Heat 3 tablespoons of the oil in a large pan and add the diced red onion, rosemary, oregano, and thyme; sauté until caramelized.
3. Dice the carrots and celery and add them to the pan, along with the sugar.
4. Pour the mince in the pan and stir vigorously, until all the ingredients are distributed evenly.

5. Once the mince is cooked, add the tomato puree.
6. Dilute the stock cube in boiling water and add to the mix.
7. Boil until the liquids are absorbed and you are left with a nice, thick sauce.
8. Take the mix off the heat and add the gruyere cheese and the egg. Mix thoroughly. Add salt and pepper to taste.
9. Grease a shallow oven-safe dish with oil or butter, and layer the first puff pastry sheet on the bottom.
10. Pour the mince mixture in the dish and cover with the remaining puff pastry sheet.
11. Score the top of the puff pastry sheet and brush it with remaining olive oil.
12. Bake for approximately 35-40 minutes, or until the pastry is golden brown.
13. Allow to cool, and enjoy!

CHICKEN GIOUVETSI
(Κοτόπουλο Γιουβέτσι)

Serves 6

Originally a dish introduced during the Ottoman Empire rule, giouvetsi (pronounced you-ve-tsee) is not a dish for the fainthearted. It is a rustic dish, full of flavor and warmth. Often prepared by my father during the cold winter nights. (Yes, it is actually cold in Greece during the winter!) I have added a few ingredients to enhance this family recipe, but it is generally very faithful to the original.

Ingredients

1 whole fresh chicken (cut into portions)

5 Tbsp. extra-virgin olive oil

1 large red onion (sliced)

2 cloves garlic (finely chopped)

2 Tbsp. tomato puree

1 leek (diced)

1 carrot (diced)

½ cup dry white wine

2 cans chopped tomatoes

1 cube chicken stock + 2 cups boiling water

2 cups orzo pasta

Salt and pepper to taste

Grated mozzarella (amount depends on taste and what your heart can handle)

Method

1. Heat some of the oil in a large pan and fry the chicken until golden brown.
2. Once the chicken has taken a nice color, add the sliced onion and garlic until caramelized.
3. Add the tomato puree, the leek, and the carrot; stir frequently in order to avoid the food sticking to the bottom of the pan.
4. When the vegetables have sautéed, pour the dry white wine and the chopped tomatoes in the pan.

5. Dissolve the chicken stock in boiling water and add to the pan. It is important that the water is boiled first, as we don't want to reduce the temperature of our food while we are cooking.

6. Add the orzo pasta in the boiling mix.

7. Add salt and pepper to taste.

8. Once all the ingredients are sufficiently cooked and the orzo has absorbed any excess liquid, remove the pan from the heat.

9. Pour the mixture from the pan into a deep oven-safe dish (preferably ceramic to keep with tradition).

10. Cover with the grated mozzarella and place it in the oven at 350°F, for approximately 20 minutes.

> **Tip:**
> Add green or red peppers or sliced mushrooms for that extra oomph!

YIOTA'S CHICKEN KEBAB
(Γύρος Κοτόπουλο)

Serves 6

Anyone who has ever visited Greece is aware of our "national fast food," the souvlaki (pronounced soo-vla-kee) and gyros (pronounced yee-ros). Traditionally served in a Greek pita bread, with tzatziki, a mixture of sliced onions, fresh flat leaf parsley, and French fries, this recipe is a deconstructed version of Greece's favorite fast food option. The fries are replaced by potato wedges, which are just as flavorsome as, if not more than, the traditional French fries. The recipe for the accompanying tzatziki dip can be found on page 94, in the "Dips" section of the book.

Ingredients

3 chicken breasts

1 cup water

½ cup olive oil

Pinch of dried oregano

2 red onions

2 tomatoes

1 bunch of flat leaf parsley

1 lemon

2 cups of Tzatziki (page 94)

6 pieces of Greek Pita Bread
   (one per portion; page 114)

Salt and pepper to taste

For the wedges

3 potatoes, cut into wedges

½ cup olive oil

Pinch of dried oregano

1 cup water

Salt and pepper to taste

Method

1. Slice the chicken breasts lengthwise into thin strips. Preheat oven to 350°F.

2. Pour water in an oven dish and place the chicken strips in, along with oil. Sprinkle with oregano, salt, and pepper, before placing in oven.

3. Bake for approximately 30 minutes.

4. Follow the same process for the potato wedges, and place in the oven.

5. While the chicken strips and the wedges are baking, slice the onions and tomatoes, and chop the flat leaf parsley for later.

6. Remove the chicken strips and potato wedges from the oven and leave to rest for 10 minutes.

7. Assemble everything on a wooden board, squeeze some lemon juice on, and enjoy!

FAMILY PORK ROAST
(Χοιρινό στη Γάστρα)

Serves 10

Sometimes there are a lot of people to be fed, especially on a Sunday, when the family descends on you because you are the only one who can cook. (Oh, the burden and responsibility!) On occasions like this, you need a strategy, and what better crowd-pleaser than a nice pork roast? This is not an exclusively Mediterranean dish; the pork roast can be found in almost every culture. However, the Greek honey and the herbs of the Greek soil give this dish an extra layer of palette-pleasing flavors. The aromas from this dish are likely to fill the corridors of your house, and if a window is left open, you might have a neighbor or two knocking at your door. Remember what I said before—this dish feeds the masses, and everyone is welcome!

Ingredients

5 large white potatoes

2 large red onions (whole)

2 carrots (diced)

3 cups mushrooms (whole or quartered)

1 large joint of pork

3 cloves garlic (sliced)

2 Tbsp. Greek honey

½ cup olive oil

2 sprigs of thyme

2 sprigs of rosemary

Pinch of oregano

1 cup water

Salt and pepper to taste

Method

1. Preheat the oven to 350°F.
2. Peel the potatoes. Don't cut them, but run your knife through the core, from one side to the other. This will allow the potato to bake evenly. Place the potatoes at the bottom of an enamel casserole dish with a lid.
3. Peel the onions and slice the carrots and, along with the whole mushrooms, place them on top of the potatoes.

4. Situate the joint of pork on the top of the concoction of vegetables and potatoes.
5. Add the garlic, honey, and oil and massage the pork joint.
6. Add the thyme, rosemary, and oregano.
7. Add the water. Cover the pot, put in the oven, and cook for approximately 2 hours.
8. Remove the lid, add salt and pepper to taste, and cook for an additional 40 minutes, to give some extra color to the roast.
9. Remove from the oven and leave to rest for 15 minutes.
10. Carve the pork joint, and serve it with the onions, potatoes, and vegetables. Enjoy!

STEAMED MUSSELS
(Μύδια Αχνιστά)

Serves 2

Mussels are popular, cheap to buy, fresh, and ultra-tasty. They are very easy to cook, and make any table look yummy with their vibrant texture and color. I remember going to the fish market with my mother when I was little. She was looking at the sea bream; I was mesmerized by the mussels. My mother wouldn't touch mussels with a bargepole; she bought into all the hype about mussels being dangerous to consume. Thankfully, years later, I grew up and I had the chance to cook midia ahnista (pronounced mee-thia ah-nee-sta). So, without further ado, let's get down to it!

Ingredients

6 cups mussels

2 Tbsp. extra-virgin olive oil

1 Tbsp. butter

2 red onions (finely chopped)

1 clove garlic (finely chopped)

1 bunch fresh flat leaf parsley

½ cup white wine

1 pinch of sugar

2 tsp. lemon juice

Pinch of sea salt and freshly ground black pepper

Method

1. Wash the mussels thoroughly with cold water and drain.
2. Heat the oil and butter in a pan and sauté the onion and garlic lightly.
3. Add the mussels and flat leaf parsley to the pan.
4. Add the wine, pinch of sugar, and lemon juice. Replace the lid, and leave to steam for 4 minutes on a high heat setting.
5. Check that the mussels have all opened up, and dispose of any unopened mussels. (Even though the danger of consuming an unopened mussel has been disproved and it is largely a myth, why take the chance?)
6. Pour the mussels on a deep plate and season with sea salt and ground black pepper. Enjoy!

MAMA VIVI'S HADDOCK WITH LEEKS

Serves 2

Fish is a very important part of the Mediterranean diet; it is nutritious, easy, quick to cook, and very tasty. When I was little, I only conceded to eating white fish with no bones, as I'd developed a fear stemming from an early encounter my throat had with a fish bone. Later on in life, I thankfully got over that fear and I got to enjoy many different types of fish, cooked in a variety of ways. This particular dish is one of my favorites, as the sauce is yummy on a piece of good bread, the potatoes satisfying, and the fish succulent and filling.

Ingredients

1 cup extra-virgin olive oil

2 red onions (sliced)

2 leeks (sliced)

2 cloves garlic

1 bunch fresh flat leaf parsley

2 ripe tomatoes (grated)

1 Tbsp. tomato puree

1 cup boiling water

3 white potatoes (peeled and sliced)

2 fillets of haddock (or cod)

Method

1. Heat the oil in a pan.
2. Add the onion, leek, and garlic, sautéing until caramelized.
3. Add the parsley and the tomatoes and leave to simmer for 5 minutes.
4. Add the tomato puree and 1 cup of boiling water; leave to simmer for a further 5 minutes.
5. Remove the pan from the heat, and preheat the oven to 350°F.
6. Layer the sliced potatoes in an ovenproof dish and pour the sauce from the pan over them.
7. Place the haddock fillets on the top and put the dish in the oven. Bake for approximately 30 minutes, or until the potatoes are cooked thoroughly and the juices are absorbed. Et voila!

Tip:
Enjoy with crumbled feta cheese and fresh bread. Just divine!

TROUT FILLET WITH SPINACH
(Γοφάρι με Σπανάκι)

Serves 2

Ingredients

2 tsp. butter
1 clove garlic (finely sliced)
2 cups baby leaf spinach
¼ cup extra-virgin olive oil
2 trout fillets

For the sauce
Juice of one lemon
½ cup extra-virgin olive oil
Pinch of oregano

Sea salt and freshly ground pepper
to taste

Method

1. In a pan, melt the butter and sauté the garlic.
2. Quickly add the baby leaf spinach, cooking just until wilted.
3. Take the pan off the fire and set aside.
4. Put a shallow frying pan on the stove and turn the heat on high. Add olive oil and immediately add the trout fillets, skin down. Do not be tempted to move the fillets around. Cook for approximately 2 minutes each side.
5. Divide the spinach on two plates and place the trout on top.
6. In a bowl add all the ingredients for the sauce, and use a fork to beat the mixture.
7. Pour on the trout and spinach and season with sea salt and freshly ground pepper. Enjoy!

Tip:
Serve with some feta cheese, olives, and freshly baked bread on the side.

SEA BREAM WITH VEGETABLES AND POTATOES
(Φαγκρί με Λαχανικά και Πατάτες)

Serves 2

A quick and easy recipe for those days that fresh food does not have to be an ordeal. Highly nutritious fillets of succulent sea bream and your 5-a-day in one dish. You can't complain!

Ingredients

½ cup extra-virgin olive oil

1 red onion (sliced)

3 ripe tomatoes (diced)

Handful of capers

Pinch of oregano

6 small potatoes

4 asparagus spears

2 sea bream fillets

Method

1. Heat the oil in a shallow pan and add the onion to caramelize.
2. Once the onion is ready, add the tomatoes and the handful of capers.
3. Add the oregano to the pan.
4. In a separate pan, boil the potatoes in salted water. When the potatoes are almost done, add the asparagus in the same water.
5. Once the sauce, the potatoes, and asparagus are done, put a separate shallow frying pan on high heat.
6. Place the sea bream fillets skin down for approximately one minute. Turn the fillets over and cook for another 2 minutes.
7. Slice the boiled potatoes, place them on a plate, and put the sea bream fillets on top. Pour a couple of tablespoons of the sauce and sprinkle some oregano. Add the asparagus and enjoy!

MOUSSAKA
(Μουσακάς)

Serves 12

The undisputed king of the Greek cuisine, moussaka! This laborious dish is worth every effort; the only drawback is that you might not get to have a piece, as it rapidly disappears as soon as it touches the dining table. Follow the steps carefully, as there are many components in this dish. It is not for the fainthearted, but once you taste it, there is no going back!

Ingredients

6 cups white potatoes

2 eggplants

3 zucchinis

2 cups olive oil, divided

2 red onions

1 clove garlic

1 Tbsp. dried oregano

1 Tbsp. fresh flat leaf parsley (finely chopped)

2 Tbsp. tomato puree

4 cups pork and beef mince (mixed)

1 can chopped tomatoes

1 cup gruyere cheese

2 Dutch crispbakes or old bread (toasted)

Salt and pepper to taste

For the béchamel sauce

1 cup butter

1 cup all-purpose flour

4 cups fresh semi-skimmed (or whole) milk

3 tsp. granulated sugar

½ tsp. ground nutmeg

1 egg yolk

Method

1. Slice the potatoes, eggplants, and zucchinis lengthwise.
2. Heat some oil in a shallow pan and fry all the vegetables in batches until golden brown, starting with the potatoes. Once cooked, place on paper towels to get rid of excess oil.
3. Proceed to prepare the mince mixture. Chop the onions and garlic finely and shallow fry them, in the pan you have just used for the vegetables, until they become translucent.

continued

4. Add the oregano, chopped parsley, and tomato puree and stir thoroughly.

5. Add the mince and ensure the meat is well mixed with the rest of the in-gredients.

6. Once the mince is cooked, add the can of chopped tomatoes and let it simmer, until cooked thoroughly. Add extra water if needed.

Assembling

8. Add half the mince mixture at the bottom of the pan; this ensures the po-tatoes do not get burned.

9. Proceed to layer the potatoes, and grate half the gruyere cheese on top.

10. Layer the eggplants, then pour the remaining half of the mince mixture on top. Layer the zucchinis, and add the rest of the grated gruyere cheese on top, keeping a handful for the top of the moussaka.

11. Preheat the oven to 350°F.

For the béchamel sauce

1. Place the butter in a deep pan and let it melt.

2. Once the butter melts, take it off the stove and gradually whisk in the flour.

3. Mix thoroughly and return to the fire to cook the flour off.

4. Once the flour is absorbed and has changed color slightly, take the pan off the heat and start adding the milk little by little, while stirring vigorously. It is important that stirring be vigorous, otherwise your sauce might turn lumpy.

5. Return to the fire and cook, still stirring, until the sauce thickens to a con-sistency thicker than custard.

6. Add the sugar and nutmeg.

7. Remove the béchamel from the heat, add the egg yolk, and stir thoroughly. The yolk will ensure your béchamel is glossy.

8. Pour the béchamel on top of the layered vegetables and mince.

9. Put the Dutch crispbakes in a food processor and turn into crumbs. Add this over the bechamel.

10. Sprinkle the gruyere cheese over the top and place in the oven for approximately 30 minutes, or until the béchamel turns a nice golden brown color. Enjoy!

Tip:
Serve with a nice refreshing Peasants' Salad (page 12). Enjoy!

PASTA PIE
(Παστίτσιο)

Serves 12

Pastitsio (pronounced pa-stee-tsee-o) is the Greek version of the western pasta bake. It is a laborious dish, due to its many parts; however, like moussaka, it is worth the trouble. It is an incredibly moreish dish, that seems to be a hit with everyone, kids especially. Traditionally, a thick long macaroni pasta would be used, but I have chosen to use tagliatelle pasta in this specific recipe, as I find it makes the pastitsio succulent and soft.

Ingredients

2 cups tagliatelle (or 4 ribbon bundles)

½ cup olive oil

1 red onion (finely chopped)

1 clove garlic (finely chopped)

2½ cups pork mince

1 tsp. tomato puree

1 can chopped tomatoes

½ bunch fresh flat leaf parsley

Pinch of oregano

2 Dutch crispbakes

3.5 oz. gruyere cheese (grated)

For the béchamel sauce

1 cup butter

1 cup all-purpose flour

4 cups fresh semi-skimmed (or whole) milk

3 tsp. granulated sugar

½ tsp. ground nutmeg

1 egg yolk

Method

1. Bring a pot of water to boil.
2. Add the tagliatelle and cook until al dente. Drain the pasta and set aside.
3. Heat the oil in a shallow pan and fry the onion and garlic until translucent.
4. Add the minced meat and stir well.
5. Once the mince is cooked, add the tomato puree, chopped tomatoes, parsley, and oregano. Simmer for ten minutes.

For the béchamel sauce

1. Melt the butter in a sauce pan over medium heat.
2. Once the butter melts, take it off the fire and gradually whisk in the flour.
3. Mix thoroughly and return to the fire to cook until flour is well-incorporated.
4. Once the flour is cooked, take the pan off the fire and start adding the milk little by little, while stirring vigorously. It is important that stirring be vigorous, otherwise your sauce might turn lumpy.
5. Add the sugar and nutmeg.
6. Return to the fire and cook, still stirring, until the sauce thickens to a consistency thicker than custard.
7. Remove the béchamel from the stove, add the egg yolk, and stir thoroughly. The yolk will ensure your béchamel is glossy.

Assembling

1. Preheat the oven to 350°F.
2. Add the tagliatelle in a deep oven dish. Layer the cooked mince on top.
3. Layer the béchamel on top of the pasta and mince mixture.
4. Put the crispbakes in a food processor and turn into crumbs. Sprinkle evenly over the dish.
5. Sprinkle the gruyere cheese on the surface and place in the oven for approximately 30 minutes, or until the béchamel turns a nice golden brown color. Enjoy!

CHICKEN BREAST WITH MEDITERRANEAN ROASTED VEGETABLES
(Μπριάμ με Κοτόπουλο)

Serves 2

I don't know about you, but there are periods of time that I have eaten way too much meat and potatoes, and I start craving vegetables. When this happens, this dish provides me with a healthy portion of vegetables that are tasty, soft, and nutritious, without the need to spend a lifetime in the kitchen. Feta cheese and warm, freshly made bread love this dish, so make sure you get your hands on some.

Ingredients

2 chicken breasts

½ cup olive oil, divided

Pinch of dried oregano

Salt and freshly ground pepper
  to taste

1 red onion (sliced)

1 garlic clove (finely chopped)

½ cup black olives

½ cup green olives

2 zucchinis

1 large eggplant

1 red pepper

2 large white potatoes

3 ripe tomatoes (grated)

3 Tbsp. Greek yogurt

Method

1. Place the chicken in an oven dish, drizzle with half the oil, sprinkle with oregano, season with salt and pepper, and fill the dish ¼ full of water before putting it in the oven at 350°F for approximately 30 minutes.

2. While the chicken is baking, heat the other half of the olive oil in a deep pan. Add the sliced onion and the finely chopped garlic and cook until translucent.

3. Slice the olives into rings and add to the pan.

4. Roughly chop the zucchinis, eggplant, pepper, and potatoes and add them to the pan also.

5. Add the grated tomatoes (canned tomatoes can be used for quickness).

6. Add approximately 2 cups of water and let the mixture simmer for approximately 20 minutes.

7. Remove the chicken breasts from the oven once they have absorbed the liquid, and set aside.

8. Remove the pan of vegetables from the fire when a thick sauce has formed and there is not a lot of liquid at the bottom of the pan.

9. Arrange the vegetables on 2 plates, lay the chicken breasts on top, and top each with a dollop of Greek yogurt.

10. Season the dishes with salt and freshly ground pepper.

HALLOUMI PITA WITH SALAD AND BLACK FOREST HAM
(Χαλουμόπιτα)

Serves 2

Light lunches do not have to be boring or flavorless. The haloumopita (pronounced ha-loo-mo-pee-ta) is a Cypriot-inspired dish, which reminds me of my second home country. There is not much cooking involved, unless you decide to follow the recipes for Greek Pita Bread and Hummus 114, 100). Keep it as simple as possible, and let the flavors do the talking. Honest, clean ingredients create the perfect marriage of flavor combinations, for your taste buds only!

Ingredients

4 pieces of Greek Pita Bread
   (page 114)

4 fresh basil leaves

2 fresh mint leaves

1 tsp. extra-virgin olive oil

1 9 oz. package halloumi cheese

8 cherry tomatoes (halved)

4 baby cucumbers (sliced)

Kalamata olives (optional)

Beetroot hummus (optional)

8 slices Black Forest ham

Olive oil to drizzle

Method

1. Preheat the oven to 350°F and heat the pita breads thoroughly (approximately 5 minutes), making sure they don't burn.

2. In a blender, mix the basil and mint leaves with the extra-virgin olive oil.

3. Slice the halloumi cheese and brush the slices with the basil and mint sauce. Place the slices on a griddle pan and cook. Turn over when golden brown.

4. Arrange the vegetables on a plate along with the beetroot hummus and Black Forest ham. Drizzle with oil.

5. Remove the pita breads from the oven, sandwich the halloumi slices between two pitas and cut into quarters. Place on the plate and enjoy!

OKRAS GIAHNI
(Μπάμιες)

Serves 4

As a kid, I would not have been seen even going near okra. I used to think they were slimy stalks of vileness. But I grew up and my palate changed, thankfully, because I now appreciate okra, its unique flavor, and its high nutritional value. Okra is an antioxidant food, which can support improvement in conditions like Type 2 diabetes and heart diseases. It contains a very high concentration of vitamin D, magnesium, and folic acid, making okra an absolute superfood!

Ingredients

4½ cups okra

Splash of red wine vinegar

2 red onions (finely sliced)

2 cloves garlic

1 cup olive oil

1 can chopped tomatoes

½ bunch fresh flat leaf parsley
   (finely chopped)

½ tsp. sugar

2 cups water

Pinch of salt and pepper

Method

1. (Skip this step if you are making this dish with frozen okra.) Chop the okra stalks off and wash thoroughly.
2. Pour the red wine vinegar over the okra and leave to stand for approximately one hour.
3. Sauté the onions and the garlic in the oil until translucent, and add the chopped tomatoes.
4. Add the okra to the pan and stir thoroughly.
5. Add the parsley, sugar, and 2 cups of water. Season to taste.
6. Simmer for approximately 30 minutes.

Tip:
Instead of using a wooden spoon to stir the okra when needed, shake the pan. This will ensure the okra does not lose its shape.

MAIN DISHES   83

BEEF STIFADO
(Μοσχάρι Στιφάδο)

Serves 3

Onions are a staple of the Greek diet, and in no other dish are they as glorious as in a heartwarming stifado (pronounced stee-fa-tho). When I was growing up, I remember my mum and dad spending hours in the kitchen preparing this fragrant dish; however, later on in life I wondered why, since it is a fairly straightforward dish to make. My guess is that they were fighting over who was going to do the dishes.

Ingredients

1 cup flour for coating

5 cups beef (diced)

1 cup olive oil, divided

½ cup wine (red or white will do)

Pinch of dried rosemary

Pinch of oregano

1½ cup tomato passata (a thick tomato juice can be used)

3 ripe tomatoes (grated)

1 bay leaf

Salt and pepper to taste

6 cups small white onions

½ cup red wine vinegar

Method

1. Flour the beef pieces.
2. Heat half of the oil in a large pan and add the floured beef, frying until golden on all sides.
3. Add the wine, rosemary, oregano, passata, grated tomatoes, bay leaf, and salt and pepper to taste. Let it simmer while you are preparing the onions.
4. In a large frying pan, use the remaining oil to sauté the onions whole, until golden brown.
5. Once the beef becomes tender, add the onions and the vinegar to the pan.
6. Simmer until the onions are soft and the sauce thickens. Enjoy!

Important note:
You can leave the salt out until the very end, as it sometimes makes the meat a bit tougher.

MUM'S STUFFED VEGETABLES
(Γεμιστά)

Serves 6

The humble gemista (pronounced ye-mee-sta) is a dish largely enjoyed by all age groups and in most seasons; however, it is traditionally a dish Greeks would make during the hotter months (which really means most of the year). It is one of the many adaptable vegetarian Greek dishes, in the sense that you can remove the cheese and make it vegan, or add pork/beef mince for the carnivore enthusiasts.

Ingredients

5 tomatoes

2 zucchinis

2 eggplants

3 green peppers

2 Tbsp. fresh flat leaf parsley (finely chopped)

1 Tbsp. fresh mint (finely chopped)

3 Tbsp. tomato puree

1½ cup olive oil, divided

1½ cups long grain rice

1 cup raisins

½ cup pine nuts

2 tsp. sugar

3 Tbsp. gouda cheese (shredded)

2 cups passata

1 red onion (finely sliced)

5 potatoes

Pinch of oregano

2 cups water

Salt and pepper to taste

Method

1. Preheat the oven to 350°F.
2. Cut off the tops of the tomatoes and scrape out the insides into a large bowl. We will be using the vegetable lids to cover the vegetables after stuffing them. Do the same for the zucchinis, eggplants, and peppers, being sure to remove the seeds. You should end up with shapes resembling boats.
3. Place the vegetable shells in a deep oven tray.

Tip:
Enjoy warm or cold with some feta cheese on the side, fresh bread, and an abundance of Greek yogurt. Enjoy!

4. Put all the vegetable flesh in a food processor and blitz lightly. You do not need to turn it into a smooth, soup-like consistency, just blitz enough for the flesh to be less lumpy.

5. Return the blitzed flesh into the large bowl and add the parsley, mint, tomato puree, ½ cup olive oil, rice, raisins, pine nuts, sugar, cheese, passata, and red onion. Use your hands to mix all the ingredients together.

6. Once the mixture is ready, start stuffing the vegetables with it. Be careful not to overstuff; leave approximately ½ inch open at the top of the vegetables, so the rice can expand while cooking.

7. Replace the vegetable lids.

8. Cut the potatoes into wedges, place them in the oven tray, and sprinkle a pinch of oregano on them.

9. Pour approximately 2 cups of water in the tray. (I know this sounds strange, but there is a method to the madness! When the potato wedges cook in the oven in a mixture of water and oil, the insides become extra fluffy and delicious.)

10. Drizzle the rest of the olive oil around the tray.

11. Season with salt and pepper to taste.

12. Bake in your preheated oven for approximately one hour.

13. Check often to see if the gemista needs more water; sometimes the rice requires more. I would check every 20 minutes or so, and baste the vegetables with the juices every time, before returning to the oven. Ensure the gemista have absorbed most of the liquid before removing from the oven.

WINE AND TOMATO CHICKEN WITH LINGUINE
(Κόκορας Κρασάτος)

Serves 6

A dish that combines alcohol and chicken—who would not get on board with that? Kokoras krasatos (pronounced ko-ko-ras kra-sa-tos) is a rich dish that satisfies the whole family. It can be served with linguine (as pictured), but it can also be accompanied with rice or French fries.

Ingredients

1 cup all-purpose flour for flouring
   the chicken

1 fresh whole chicken (cut into
   portions)

1 cup olive oil, divided

2 red onions (sliced)

2 garlic cloves (finely chopped)

1 bay leaf

4 tomatoes

1 tsp. tomato puree

1 chicken stock cube

1 cup dry red wine

2½ cups boiling water

1 tsp. sugar

1 16 oz. packet of linguine pasta

Method

1. Put the flour in a bag (plastic or paper will do). Add the chicken portions and shake well.

2. Heat half of the oil in a large pan, and add the chicken portions until golden brown. Remove the chicken portions and set aside. Dispose of the oil used in this process.

3. Heat the other half of the oil in a new pan, add the onions and garlic, cooking until translucent. Add the bay leaf.

4. Add the chicken pieces and cook for approximately 5 minutes.

5. While the chicken is getting acquainted with the onions, the garlic, and the bay leaf, grate the tomatoes into a bowl, along with the tomato puree and the chicken stock cube. Add 2½ cups of boiling water and stir.

6. Pour the wine in the frying pan and add the tomato mixture. Add the sugar, turn the heat down, and allow to simmer for 25 minutes.

7. The flour on the surface of the chicken will help the sauce to thicken, leaving a scrumptious tomato sauce. Be careful, as the chicken will stick to the bottom and burn quite quickly. It is important that you do not leave this pan unattended.

8. In a separate pan, boil some water and add the linguine.

9. Once the linguine is cooked, drain and place on a large platter.

10. Add the chicken portions with a generous amount of the sauce on top.

Tip:
Traditionally, this food would be served with a sprinkle of *mizithra* (pronounced mee-zee-thra) cheese. This is quite hard to source outside Greece, so use any hard, white cheese you can find and enjoy!

LINGUINE WITH HOMEMADE PESTO
(Λινγκουίνι με Σπιτικό Πέστο)

Ingredients

1 large bunch of fresh basil

3 garlic cloves (without the germ)

4 Tbsp. pine nuts

1 cup grated parmesan

1 cup extra-virgin olive oil

Salt and pepper to taste

1 16 oz. packet of linguine pasta

Tools

Pestle and mortar (or blender)

Method

1. Put the basil leaves and the garlic in the mortar and grind them until they form a paste.
2. Add the pine nuts, the parmesan, and the oil. Use the pestle to bring all the ingredients together into the consistency of a paste.
3. Salt and pepper to taste.
4. Boil the linguine to desired doneness, and drain.
5. Arrange the pasta on a plate and pour a generous amount of pesto on top. Enjoy!

DIPS

One of my best memories of Greece, and one of the memories shared by in-laws that have traveled with me to my hometown, is of sitting on a balcony or a terrace and enjoying the sea view with a drink of ouzo and a mezze.

Ouzo is hard alcohol, and whenever this is served in a café it's always accompanied by a small selection of dips, cured meats, cheeses, and other finger food. These foods are also ordered with glasses of wine and even cups of Greek coffee. It's a great way to unwind in the evening and enjoy a light supper with friends.

Some of the dips in this section are inspired by those cafés and tavern creations. It's party food, finger food; it's food to enjoy with alcohol, as well as food to enjoy as a light brunch.

I always like to have a pot of hummus or tzatziki in the fridge and there is usually some freshly made pita on hand as well. That way, whenever I'm looking for a quick bite to eat, I just grab a quick scoop and stay away from the chocolate, the sweets, and the other things I may otherwise reach for.

These dips require a few basic ingredients and a little preparation, and if you make a big batch, they will usually stay good for up to a week in the fridge.

Mother on garlic: «Το μυστικό για καλό τζατζίκι είναι ο άνηθος. Το μυστικό για όλα τα υπόλοιπα φαγητά είναι το σκόρδο»

"The secret ingredient to tzatziki is dill. The secret ingredient to everything else is garlic."

TZATZIKI
(Τζατζίκι)

Serves 4 to 6 as a starter

As far as my granddad was concerned, if you didn't like garlic, you were either a vampire or of a weak disposition. A staple of Greek cuisine, this world-famous dip has suffered many variations through the years. No, it is not about grating some cucumber and mixing it with Greek yogurt! Tzatziki is the result of the fine balance of the ingredients which comprise it. It is a dream on pita bread or focaccias, or just as an accompaniment to a main meal. There is no cooking involved, so one can enjoy a guilt-free, delicious tzatziki in just ten minutes. The most important thing to remember is that you need the best quality ingredients possible for the tzatziki to be at its tastiest. The cucumber's juices will need to be strained, in order to avoid a watery tzatziki.

Ingredients

1 large cucumber

2½ cups strained Greek yogurt

4 cloves of garlic

2 Tbsp. extra-virgin olive oil (the higher the quality, the better)

1 small bunch of fresh dill

Salt to taste

Method

1. Peel the cucumber and grate it on the medium grate. Place the grated cucumber in a sieve or on some paper towels and wring tightly.
2. Add the cucumber to the Greek yogurt and mix well.
3. Peel the garlic and grate it finely. Mix with the olive oil and add to the yogurt. Stir well.
5. Chop the dill and fold into the yogurt mixture. Salt to taste.
6. Serve with warm pita or regular bread, or just as an accompaniment to your main meal.

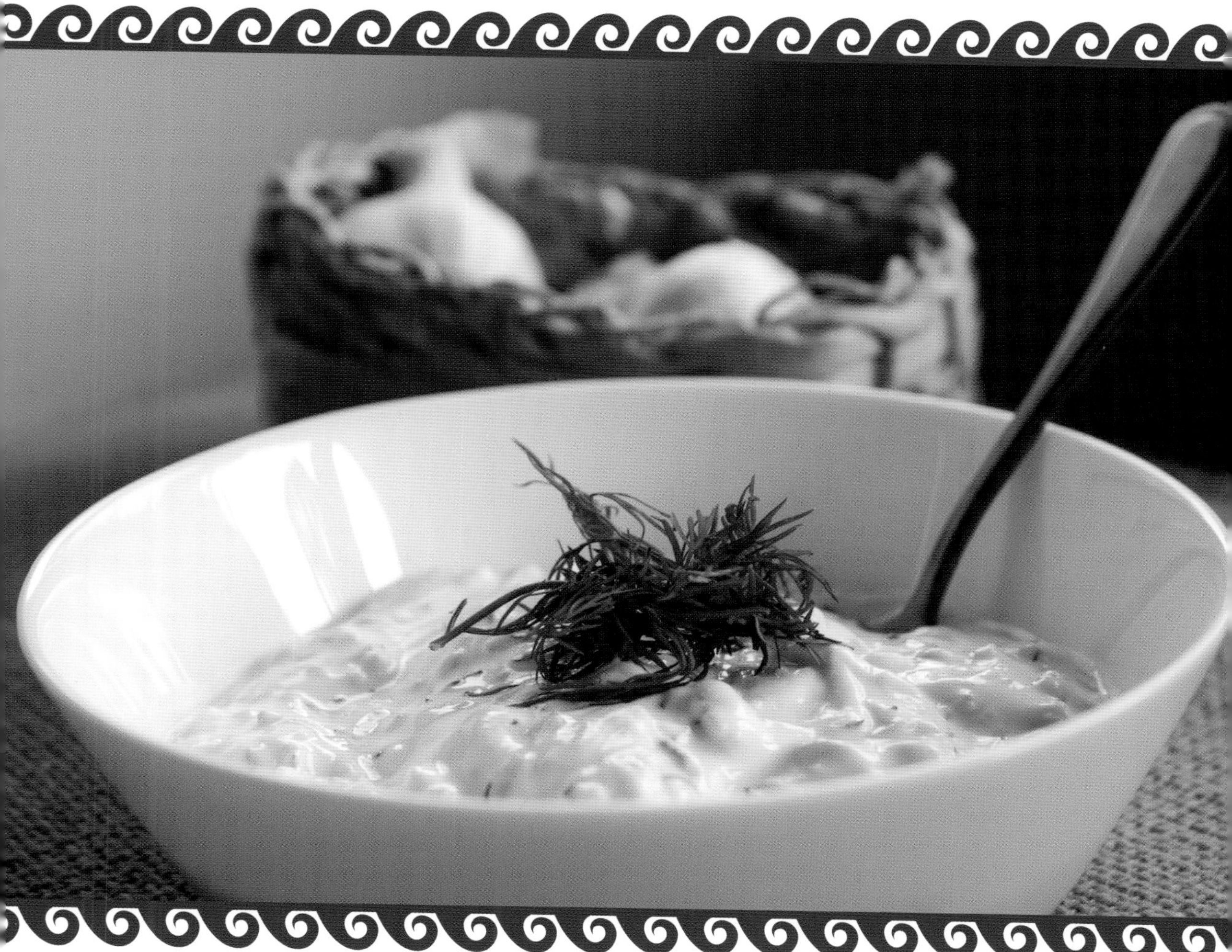

EGGPLANT DIP
(Μελιτζανοσαλάτα)

A dip dear to the Greek heart, melitzanosalata (pronounced me-lee-ja-no-sa-la-ta) is the side dish of choice to accompany almost every meal, especially during the summer months. Its roots are Middle Eastern, thus it's related to its cousin the Levantine baba ghanoush. This no-frills version is exposing the amazing taste of the raw ingredients used. A quick and easy recipe, full of flavor. It's amazing!

Ingredients

4 large eggplants
1 large red onion (finely grated)
2 garlic cloves (finely grated)
1 cup extra-virgin olive oil
Juice of two large lemons
1 bunch fresh flat leaf parsley
Salt and pepper to taste

Method

1. Cover a shallow baking tray with baking parchment and place the eggplants whole on the surface.
2. Bake at 350°F, for approximately 20 minutes, or until the eggplants are soft.
3. Remove the eggplants from the oven and place on a cooling rack.
4. Place the onion, garlic, olive oil, lemon juice, and flat leaf parsley in a blender and pulse to combine.
5. Once the eggplants have cooled down, mash them using a fork and add the mixture from your blender.
6. Mix the ingredients until every ingredient is distributed evenly.
7. Salt and pepper to taste.

Tip:
Add roasted red peppers, chili, and cumin to the mixture to jazz up the dip!

YELLOW SPLIT PEA DIP
(Φάβα)

Serves 6 as a starter

A staple of the Greek diet—the humble yellow split pea. In the past, the yellow split pea singlehandedly provided sustenance to many a poor Greek island resident; this is the main reason why "fava" is the national dish as far as the islands of Cyclades are concerned. The best yellow split pea comes from the island of Santorini; it is coarser than the yellow split pea one can buy in the supermarket. This humble food has many gastronomical possibilities, but it is at its best when it accompanies dishes that include fish and seafood.

Ingredients

1 cup extra-virgin olive oil
2 large red onions
1 lb. dried yellow split peas
Juice of two lemons

Method

1. Heat the olive oil in an average-sized sauce pan.
2. Chop one of the onions into quarters and place in the pan to sauté.
3. Once golden brown, add the yellow split peas with enough boiling water to fill half the pan.
4. Leave to boil until soft.
5. Once softened, remove from the heat and blend until a smooth paste forms. (You can use an immersion blender, or transfer the mixture to a traditional blender.)
6. Serve with good quality extra-virgin olive oil, lemon juice, and a sliced onion.

Tip:
Add chopped flat
leaf parsley and
capers for a taste
with a kick!

HUMMUS
(Χούμους)

Serves 6

Sesame seeds, chickpeas, paprika, and everything that smells nice in this world! This quick and easy recipe will allow you to enjoy this explosion of taste, which accompanies a myriad of different dishes. However, my personal preference is to have hummus with freshly baked bread or pita, on its own.

Ingredients

4 Tbsp. tahini (sesame paste)

2 lemons (juiced)

2 cups boiled chickpeas (canned will also do and reduces the time considerably)

3 cloves of garlic (crushed)

½ tsp. cumin

1 tsp. salt

5 Tbsp. extra-virgin olive oil

3 Tbsp. water

½ bunch of fresh flat leaf parsley (finely chopped)

Pinch of paprika

Method

1. Using a blender, blend the tahini and lemon juice until the ingredients are homogenized.
2. Add the chickpeas and blend again, until you are left with a thick paste.
3. Add the garlic, cumin, and salt to the mix; blend further.
4. Start adding the olive oil to the hummus gradually, and mix together until well-incorporated.
5. Add the water. You might need to add a bit more depending on how thick you prefer your hummus to be.
6. Serve with chopped flat leaf parsley, a drizzle of extra-virgin olive oil, and a pinch of paprika.

Tip:
Roast some red peppers in the oven and add to the blender in Step 2. Sweeeeeet!

FETA CHEESE AND SWEET RED PEPPER DIP
(Ντίπ με Φέτα και Κόκκινη Πιπεριά)

Serves 4

Ingredients

4 sweet red peppers
1½ cups of feta cheese
2 Tbsp. extra-virgin olive oil
1 tsp. dried oregano
Salt and pepper to taste

Method

1. Place the peppers on a shallow oven tray and bake at 350°F for approximately 20 minutes, or until softened.
2. Remove the peppers from the oven, put them in a plastic bag, and let them cool down; this will make removing their skin easier.
3. Remove the pepper skin, and chop the peppers into tiny cubes. (Let's get those knife skills going!)
4. In a food processor, blend the feta cheese, the oil, and the oregano, until the mixture is homogenized.
5. Add half the tiny pepper cubes and blitz slightly.
6. Pour the mixture in a bowl and fold the remaining pepper cubes into it.
7. Salt and pepper to taste and serve with warm pita bread. Enjoy!

SWEET RED PEPPER SALSA DIP
(Σάλσα Κόκκινης Πιπεριάς)

Serves 4

Ingredients

4 sweet red peppers
2 garlic cloves (finely grated)
1 tsp. dried oregano
2 Tbsp. red wine vinegar
2 Tbsp. extra-virgin olive oil
3 Tbsp. fresh flat leaf parsley
Salt and pepper to taste

Method

1. Place the peppers on a shallow oven tray and bake at 350°F for approximately 20 minutes, or until softened.
2. Remove the peppers from the oven, put them in a plastic bag, and let them cool down; this will make removing their skin easier.
3. Remove the skins and chop the peppers into tiny cubes. (Let's get those knife skills going!)
4. Add the garlic, oregano, oil, and vinegar.
5. Fold all the ingredients until well mixed.
6. Sprinkle the flat leaf parsley.
7. Salt and pepper to taste.

Tip:
Accompany with a glass of red wine and crusty bread. Bliss!

HARISSA DIP
(Ντίπ με Χαρίσα)

Serves 6

A dip not for the fainthearted. Its Moroccan origins give this dip its rich red color and almighty kick. Serve with strong meats like lamb and beef, and you will not regret it. It is also a great accompaniment to the Eggplant Dip (page 96).

Ingredients

6 sweet red peppers

1 cup extra-virgin olive oil

2 tsp. salt

Pinch of sugar

2 Tbsp. chili (ground or flakes)

1 tsp. cayenne pepper

1 tsp. ground black pepper

Method

1. Remove the seeds from the peppers and boil for approximately 10 minutes, or until they are soft enough for the skin to be removed.

2. Blend the skinned peppers until a smooth paste forms.

3. Put the paste in a small pan and add the olive oil, salt, sugar, chili, cayenne, and black pepper.

4. Leave to simmer on low heat. Stir often to avoid the harissa sticking to the bottom of the pan.

5. When the mixture looks homogenized, remove from the stove and set aside to cool.

6. Once the harissa cools down, store in glass jars and refrigerate.

SESAME PASTE
(Ταχίνι)

Tahini (*pronounced ta-hee-nee*) is the nectar of the gods; a paste used for one of the most incredibly delicious dishes around, hummus. You'll find my hummus recipe on page 100, which requires you to have made this superfood paste first. There are other ways to enjoy tahini, of course; you can use it as a spread on some toasted bread and drizzle it with honey, or you can use it as a salad dressing, or even a dip. You can buy tahini ready-made in jars, but my motto is "Nothing beats homemade!"

Ingredients

5 cups sesame seeds
1½ Tbsp. extra-virgin olive oil
Salt to taste

Method

1. Toast the sesame seeds on a high heat, using a large frying pan. Do not use oil, sesame has enough natural oils to aid this process. Stir often and take care not to burn these potent but sensitive seeds. Remove the seeds when they have slightly changed in color. Don't over-toast them, as they can taste bitter. Once the seeds are ready, move onto a dish and let them cool down.

2. Put the seeds into a blender and blend for two minutes, until they form a thick paste.

3. Add a bit of the extra-virgin olive oil and the salt, and blend until homogenized. Keep adding olive oil, until the desired "gluey" consistency is achieved.

4. Pour the tahini paste into jars and refrigerate. Tahini paste lasts for many months. Just keep blending the oil that surfaces to the top back into the paste, just before use.

GRANDDAD GEORGIOS'S GARLIC POTATOES
(Σκορδαλιά)

Serves 6

No dish reminds me of my Granddad Georgios more than the skordalia (pronounced skor-tha-lia). Garlic was always adorning the table, no matter what the main dish was. Almost the opposite of Dracula, he used to announce "Garlic is life!" And he was quite right. Garlic has a lot of antioxidant properties, and ensures your ticker is healthy.

Ingredients

4 cups potatoes (cut into small chunks)

½ cup extra-virgin olive oil

½ cup white wine vinegar

3 garlic cloves

1 tsp. sea salt

Freshly ground pepper

3 Tbsp. fresh flat leaf parsley

2 green onions (sliced)

Method

1. Bring a pot of salted water to a rolling boil. Add the potatoes and boil for approximately 25 minutes.
2. Combine in a blender the olive oil, vinegar, garlic, salt, and freshly ground pepper.
3. Once the potatoes have softened, drain the excess liquid and let the potatoes cool for about 5 minutes.
4. Use a potato masher to roughly mash the potatoes.
5. Pour the mixture from the blender on the potatoes and stir well.
6. Sprinkle the flat leaf parsley and the green onion and serve.

Tip:
You can replace the potatoes with stale bread soaked in water for a more authentic taste.

BREADS

There is always bread on a Greek dinner table, whether to soak up the oil or the sauce; to nibble on before the main course arrives; or to enjoy with a selection of dips. Bread is a key ingredient in a small number of dishes found throughout this book, but it's something that always provides a welcome accompaniment.

In Greece, we never eat sandwiches. "Sandwich bread" is firmer and dryer, and that's because what we call a "sandwich" is more akin to the American "grilled cheese sandwich" or the British "toastie." In other words, it's always grilled and served hot.

The bread we serve at the dinner table is also firmer and dryer. In the UK, and indeed across northern Europe, the bread tends to be very soft and dense, and that's something you just won't find in Greece or across the Mediterranean. The bread in this section is all made the traditional Greek way. We use olive oil instead of animal fat, we don't add too much sugar or salt, and we knead it until it is light and fluffy.

Most of this bread is obviously best served fresh after it has cooled, but if you have a little left over the next day, then get out the dips. If there are still some slices left on day three, it will go well with a high quality olive oil or balsamic vinegar. Just cut little bits off, dip them in, and enjoy!

Elena on Greek salad: «Δε θέλω φαγητό σήμερα. Έλα να φάμε μια χωριάτικη με μπόλικο ψωμί για να βουτήξουμε».

"I don't feel like eating a main meal today. Let's eat a salad with copious amounts of bread to dip in the oil."

GREEK PITA BREAD
(Πίτα)

Traditionally used to wrap souvlaki and gyros (recipe for chicken kebabs on page 60), the pita can accompany a plethora of dishes. So, let's get down to it!

Ingredients

1 dried yeast sachet

1 tsp. sugar

1 cup fresh whole milk

½ cup water

1½ cups all-purpose flour (or bread flour)

½ tsp. salt

2 Tbsp. olive oil

Pinch of pepper

Method

1. Mix the yeast and sugar with the milk and water in a small bowl, stirring until homogenized.
2. In a large bowl, combine the flour and the salt. Add the wet mixture and bring the ingredients together, using your hands.
3. Rub some oil on the dough and cover the bowl with plastic wrap. Leave in a warm place to rise for approximately 40 minutes, until it is approximately double its original size.
4. When the dough has risen, remove from the bowl and place on your counter top.
5. Divide the dough into 8 equal pieces, flour your work surface, and use a rolling pin to form 8 circular disks. Sprinkle with a pinch of pepper.
6. Heat a small drop of oil in a frying pan and cook the pita breads for 1½ minutes each side, until golden brown.

Tip:
Pita breads love tzatziki and any kind of dip! Enjoy!

HALLOUMI PIE
(Χαλλουμωτή)

Ingredients

1½ cups all-purpose flour

½ Tbsp. granulated sugar

½ tsp. salt

1 sachet dried yeast

¼ cup extra-virgin olive oil

½ cup water

½ cup lukewarm milk

Zest of one lemon

2 16 oz. halloumi cheese blocks, cubed

4 Tbsp. fresh mint (finely chopped)

2 eggs (beaten)

1 cup sesame seeds

Method

1. Sift the flour into a bowl and add the sugar and salt.
2. Add the dried yeast and stir thoroughly.
3. Add the olive oil and combine until it is absorbed in the flour and distributed throughout.
4. Add the water and milk, and knead the dough until it is soft and elastic.
5. Cover for approximately 60 minutes.
6. Once the dough has doubled in size, split the dough in two equal parts and roll into thin circular shapes.
7. Add the lemon zest, halloumi cheese, and mint, then form each piece into a roll as long as your baking tray, and cut each roll into four pieces.
8. Place the pieces onto a large shallow oven tray and egg-wash the surface.
9. Sprinkle evenly with sesame seeds.
10. Bake at 350°F for approximately 40 minutes, until golden brown. Enjoy!

LAGANA BREAD
(Λαγάνα)

Makes 2 large laganas

The lagana (pronounced la-ya-na) is a staple of the Greek tradition for the start of Lent. The first day of Lent is called Clean Monday, and like every Greek tradition, religious or not, it revolves around food. That one day a year, Greek families roam the countryside, with their picnic baskets and their kites at hand. Typically, foods consumed on Clean Monday would include squid, octopus, olives, fish roe dip, and lagana. Traditionally, lagana would not include yeast, but the modern version ensures that this fantabulous bread is soft and satisfying.

Ingredients

1½ cups lukewarm water (careful, if the water is hot and not warm it will kill the yeast)

1 sachet dried yeast

2 Tbsp. granulated sugar

2½ cups all-purpose flour

1 tsp. salt

¾ cup extra-virgin olive oil

¾ cup sesame seeds

Method

1. Pour the lukewarm water in a measuring jug and add the yeast and half of the sugar. Leave for 5 minutes until little foaming bubbles start appearing on the top.

2. Sift the flour into a large bowl along with the salt, and mix well to distribute the salt. Make a little well in the middle of the flour and add the activated yeast from Step 1, along with the olive oil. Mix thoroughly by hand or by using a dough hook. As soon as the dough is ready, put in on a floured work surface. Knead the dough thoroughly, until the dough is soft and elastic. When ready, brush some oil in a bowl and place the dough inside. Cover with plastic wrap and leave in a warm place for an hour and thirty minutes, until it doubles in size.

3. Once that process is done, preheat the oven to 350°F. Get the dough and cut it in two equal parts. Manipulate the dough on a shallow oven tray into a thin oblong shape, much like you would do for a pizza. Using your fingers, put deep holes on the surface of the oblong-shaped dough (use force, some of the holes need to pierce to the other side of the dough). Repeat the process for the other piece of dough.

4. Brush the laganas with olive oil and sprinkle with sesame seeds.

5. Bake for approximately 30 minutes, and enjoy!

Tip:
If you spray some water on the laganas approximately five minutes before they are due to come out of the oven, they will develop a nice glossy sheen.

BLACK OLIVE BREAD
(Ελιόψωμο)

Ahhhh, the eliopsomo (pronounced e-lee-o-pso-mo)! Many people have a love/hate relationship with olives, but olive bread is not about using an overwhelming amount of olives. Rather, it is about the balance of several ingredients, which produces a rustic bread worthy of accompanying a variety of dishes such as soups and dips.

Ingredients

1 sachet dried yeast

1½ cups lukewarm water

1 Tbsp. honey

3 cups all-purpose flour

1 cup Greek yogurt

2 Tbsp. olive oil

1½ cups butter

1 tsp. sugar

1 tsp. salt

1 cup black olives (sliced into rings)

½ cup feta cheese (crumbled)

1 egg (beaten)

3 Tbsp. sesame seeds

Method

1. Mix the yeast with the lukewarm water and the honey. Leave for approximately 10 minutes, until foaming bubbles appear on the surface.

2. In a deep mixing bowl, add the flour and the yeast mixture, yogurt, oil, butter, sugar, and salt, and mix thoroughly.

3. On a floured bench surface, knead the dough vigorously for approximately 10 minutes.

4. Let the dough rest in a bowl for approximately 20 minutes.

5. Once the dough is rested, preheat the oven to 350°F. Cut the dough into four parts and sprinkle with the chopped olives and feta cheese. Proceed to create any shape you would like. One of the most popular shapes for eliopsomo is that of a plait.

6. Place on a baking tray, brush the surface with the egg, and sprinkle some sesame seeds.

7. Bake approximately 35 minutes.

SEEDED BREAD WITH SULTANAS AND RAISINS
(Πολύσπορο Ψωμί με Μαύρες Σταφίδες και Σουλτανίνες)

Heaven is walking in an artisan bakery and being surrounded by different aromas, shapes, sizes, types, flavors, and textures of bread. When you put this recipe in the oven, your house will smell divine. It is no wonder estate agents advise landlords to use this very smell for open house days or private viewings. It is the homiest smell you can ask for. My grandma used to make sourdough bread, and bake it in a wood burning clay oven. It is still to this day the best bread I have ever tasted. This is my take on the traditional one, which I enjoy immensely.

Ingredients

2½ cups all-purpose flour (plus extra for dusting)

1 sachet fast-action yeast

2 tsp. sugar

2 tsp. salt

3 Tbsp. olive oil

1½ cups warm water

A handful of pumpkin, sunflower, linseed, and sesame seeds

A handful of crushed walnut

A handful of raisins and sultanas

Method

1. Pour the flour in a mixer bowl along with the yeast, sugar, and salt. Mix with a wooden spoon.
2. Add the oil and the water into the mix.
3. Add the seeds, nuts, raisins, and sultanas.
4. Mix with a dough hook for approximately 5 minutes.
5. Remove the mixer bowl, cover with plastic wrap, and place in a warm place for approximately one hour.

6. Once the dough has risen, knead the dough on a floured work area for 5 minutes.

7. Put the dough back in the mixing bowl, re-cover, and let sit for another hour.

8. Preheat the oven to 350°F. Once the dough has risen again, place it on an oven tray and shape into a circular shape. Bake for approximately 40 minutes.

9. Remove from the oven, and wrap with a damp kitchen towel for ten minutes.

Tip:
Slice and enjoy warm with butter and jam.

SWEETS

The more you abstain, the more tempted you will be.

I don't think there is anything wrong with a few sweet desserts every now and then and that's why I have included this section. Everyone knows it's a special occasion when the pastries and cakes show up, and I think we all need to feel that childish delight every now and then. Desserts are often cooked for special occasions in Greece. We make cakes, cream pies, and other treats for birthdays and celebrations, and we cook sweets loaded with syrup, nuts, and pastry when we have guests or when we're celebrating New Year's Day, Christmas, or Easter.

In Greece, desserts are one of the few things that we do buy in. My father is a big fan of a local cake shop, but even he would prefer a home cooked dessert, and if you have the time it's always worth the extra effort to make it yourself.

So, while I wouldn't recommend eating the desserts in this section on a regular basis, they make for a great alternative to store-bought cakes during special occasions.

After all, it's still scratch-cooking and there is still very little reliance on processed ingredients.

Pappou Georgios on wine: «Το καλό φαί χρειάζεται λίπος και ένα ποτήρι κρασί».

"Good food always needs a little fat and a glass of wine."

CREAM-FILLED FILO PASTRY PIE—BOUGATSA
(Μπουγάτσα)

Serves 8

Native to Northern Greece, this creamy delight has always been one of my favorite sweets and it is suitable for every occasion. I often prepare it as a sweet, but in Greece it is traditionally eaten as a breakfast, much like a Danish or a croissant. It goes great with a cup of Greek coffee, and can be enjoyed as a snack any time.

Ingredients

1 cup butter

2 packs filo pastry

1 cup granulated sugar

4 eggs + 2 yolks

1 tsp. vanilla extract

1 tsp. baking powder

2 cups fresh milk

2 cups double cream

3 Tbsp. Demerara sugar

Powdered sugar and cinnamon
   (for dusting before serving)

Methods

1. Preheat the oven to 400°F.
2. Melt the butter in the microwave or in a small pan on the stove.
3. Lightly grease a shallow oven pan with the butter we've just melted.
4. Layer 4 pastry sheets on the shallow pan, lightly greasing one sheet at a time with the butter.
5. Ensure that you drizzle each sheet with melted butter, prior to folding it. Carefully fold each individual remaining pastry sheet, into an overlapping shape that resembles the bellows of an accordion. Stack the sheets next to each other, on top of the existing sheets in the pan.
6. Place in the oven for 20 minutes, until the filo turns golden brown.

7. Prepare the crème Anglaise by beating the granulated sugar with the eggs and yolks in a large bowl, until the sugar dissolves.

8. Add the vanilla extract, baking powder, milk, and double cream. Mix the ingredients really well until the sugar dissolves.

9. Remove the filo from the oven and pierce the filo lightly with the tip of a knife to allow the cream to seep into the crevices. Pour the crème Anglaise all over the pastry.

10. Sprinkle some Demerara sugar and place back in the oven for another 15 minutes. Once the cream has cooked, remove the pan from the oven and leave it to cool down.

11. Using a sieve, dust the top of your bougatsa with powdered sugar and cinnamon.

HARD CHRISTMAS COOKIES
(Κουραμπιέδες)

Makes a batch of 30 cookies

Kourampiedes *(pronounced coo-ra-bie-thes)* are an integral part of the Greek Christmas tradition. Along with the Melomakarona (page 138), these are the two sweets you will never see missing from a Greek house during the winter holiday. Problem is, they disappear fast, so you have to make haste and maybe even lock them in a cupboard at night! These balls of yumminess will leave you wanting more… and more… and more.

Ingredients

1½ cups butter, room temperature

½ cup margarine, room temperature

½ cup powdered sugar

⅓ cup brandy

½ tsp. nutmeg

1 tsp. baking soda

2 tsp. vanilla extract

1 cup roasted almonds (coarsely chopped)

3½ cups soft white flour

Zest of 1 orange

2 Tbsp. rose water

Powdered sugar (for dusting)

Method

1. Place the butter and the margarine in a mixer and beat at the highest speed setting for 5 minutes, until creamy.

2. Lower the speed setting and add the powdered sugar, brandy, nutmeg, baking soda, vanilla, and the roasted almonds.

3. Sift the flour and gradually fold it into the mixture gently, using a spatula. Return to the mixer; mix for another 5 minutes on a high speed setting, and a further 5 minutes on a low speed setting, until the ingredients are well blended and the mixture becomes light and fluffy.

4. Add the orange zest.

5. Once the mixture is ready, divide it into little oblong cookie balls.
6. Preheat the oven to 350°F.
7. Place a sheet of baking parchment on a baking tray, and distribute the cookies evenly.
8. Bake for approximately 30 minutes, or until golden brown.
9. Remove from the oven and spray with rose water.
10. Sift a thick layer of powdered sugar on the cookies and display on your festive table.

Tip:
If you have a K-beater attachment, you can use this after Step 1 for a fluffier mixture.

FRIED FILO PASTRY BITES IN SYRUP
(Κουρκουμπίνια)

So, kourkoumpinia (*pronounced koo-rkoo-bee-nia*). I know this is supposed to be a health-conscious book, and that fried dough seems out of place. I tend to agree with what my ancient ancestors used to say, *"Everything in moderation,"* which I interpret as *"If you don't want to be unhealthy, do not eat a whole batch of kourkoumpinia."* This kind of sweet is very popular in Greece, where syrup takes pride of place with regards to traditional sweets, etc. These little bites of awesomeness might even make you forget chocolate! Maybe… hmm… maybe not.

Ingredients

1 packet of filo pastry sheets
½ cup butter, melted, for brushing
Oil for frying

For the syrup

1 lemon
3 cups granulated sugar
2 cups water
2 Tbsp. vanilla extract
½ tsp. ground cinnamon

Method

1. Brush two of the pastry sheets with butter and roll lengthwise into a tight, long, thin sausage shape. Brush the long edges with water, for a better "seal," otherwise the kourkoumpinia might lose their shape. Repeat until no filo pastry sheets are left.
2. Place the rolls in the fridge for one hour.
3. Remove the rolls from the fridge and cut into little bite sizes, approximately 1½ inches wide.
4. Heat the oil and add the kourkoumpinia, frying until golden brown.
5. Remove from the pan and rest on paper towels until all the oil is absorbed.

6. Peel the lemon, using a vegetable peeler. It does not matter what size the strips are.

7. Mix sugar, water, vanilla, and cinnamon in a medium pan and add the lemon peel along with 1 teaspoon of lemon juice. Bring to a boil and cook for approximately 7 minutes.

8. Once the syrup is ready, drench the kourkoumpinia and let them absorb it. Enjoy!

GREEK DOUGHNUTS
(Λουκουμάδες)

Makes a batch of 40

Loukoumades (*pronounced loo-koo-ma-thes*) were literally the food of champions in Ancient Greece. Around 776 BCE, when the first ever Olympic Games took place, gold medalists were rewarded with an offer of these delightful little honey balls of sunshine. Allegedly, the first textbook mention ever of any baking product in the history of Europe was that of loukoumades. Many Ancient Greek texts refer to loukoumades as the "delightful disks of joy." In homage to that early ritual for champions, loukoumades were also offered to the gold medalists in the 2008 Olympic Games in Beijing. So, let's get down to it!

Ingredients

For the dough balls

1 cup water

1 cup lukewarm milk

2 sachets dry yeast

1 tsp. sugar

1 tsp. salt

1 Tbsp. olive oil

1 cup all-purpose flour

1 cup self-rising flour

For frying

4 cups of canola oil

For garnishing

Powdered sugar

1 cup honey

½ chocolate praline

Method

1. In a deep mixing bowl, pour the water and lukewarm milk.

2. In a separate bowl, mix the yeast and the sugar and add them to the wet mix. Add the salt and olive oil and blend everything together.

3. Gradually add the flours to the wet mix, stirring vigorously. The mixture's consistency should be a bit thicker than that for pancakes, but not too thick.

4. Leave the mixture to rise in a warm place for approximately 40 minutes, until little bubbles are visible on the surface.

5. Heat the oil in a large pan. Using a spoon, take a small bit from the mixture and drop in in the hot oil. It should naturally form a ball, or a shape near that. Repeat the process until no mix is left. You need to be fast when turning the loukoumades in the frying pan, as they will cook quite fast; 2 minutes are usually enough. It might help to dip the spoon in some water before dipping it back in the mixture.

6. Put some paper towels on a plate to place the loukoumades. Remove the loukoumades from the pan, using a spider strainer or a skimmer.

7. Pour some honey, melted chocolate praline, and powdered sugar on top.

Tip:
Sprinkle some finely chopped walnuts on top for that extra oomph!

TWICE-BAKED GREEK STYLE BISCOTTI
(Παξιμάδια)

Ingredients

¾ cup extra-virgin olive oil + 2 Tbsp. for greasing

¾ cup red wine

½ cup orange juice

1 cup sugar

1 cup raisins

1 cup sultanas

2 tsp. fennel seeds

½ tsp. ground cinnamon

½ tsp. ground cloves

2 cups all-purpose flour

½ tsp. baking soda

4 tsp. baking powder

1 tsp. orange peel

Sesame seeds for sprinkling

Method

1. Preheat oven to 350°F.
2. Mix all the wet ingredients except 2 Tbsp. olive oil in a large bowl.
3. Add the sugar, raisins, sultanas, fennel seeds, and spices, and stir vigorously.
4. Add half the flour, with the baking soda, baking powder, and orange peel, and stir until the ingredients are mixed well.
5. Add the rest of the flour until a stiff dough is formed.
6. Coat a large baking sheet with 2 tablespoons olive oil. Split the dough into two equal parts and form each piece into a roll as long as your baking tray.
7. Cut the rolls into inch-wide pieces and separate slightly.

8. Sprinkle enough sesame seeds to cover the top of the biscotti.

9. Bake for approximately 50 minutes.

10. Take the biscotti out and separate with a knife, lay the biscotti on their sides, and bake again for another 10 minutes.

11. Remove from the oven and rest on a cooling rack for 20 minutes.

Hot tip:
Enjoy with a freshly brewed cup of coffee!

RAVANI
(Ραβανί)

Serves 12

This dish can be found in many Middle Eastern cultures; some call it ravani (pro-nounced ra-va-nee), others call it basbousa, and other call it shamali. The citrus flavors delivered by the orange and lemon peel ensure this quick and easy sweet will be established as one of your go-to recipes instantly. This semolina cake is covered in luscious sweet syrup and served with ice cream.

Ingredients

1½ cup all-purpose flour

2 cups semolina flour

3 tsp. baking powder

1 cup butter, softened

½ cup sugar

5 eggs

Orange and lemon zest

½ tsp. baking soda

1 Tbsp. vanilla extract

½ cup ground pistachio nuts

For the syrup

3 cups granulated sugar

4 cups water

1 cinnamon stick

Orange peel

Method

1. In a large bowl, sift the all-purpose flour and add the semolina and baking powder.
2. In a mixer, place the butter and the sugar and beat until the mixture is pale and homogenized. Add the eggs, orange and lemon zest, baking soda, and vanilla extract.
3. Gradually add the flour mixture, while continuing to mix.
4. Preheat the oven to 350°F.
5. Butter a 9 x 13-inch baking dish and pour the mixture in.
6. Bake for approximately 45 minutes, or until golden brown.

7. While the mixture is baking, start preparing the syrup by mixing all the syrup ingredients in a sauce pan. Boil for approximately 10 minutes. Once ready, set aside to cool.

8. Remove the baking pan from the oven, score the ravani into little rhombuses, and pour the syrup on, making sure it is equally distributed. Do not worry if it appears as though the syrup is too much and the ravani is soaking; in approximately 10 minutes, there will be no syrup left as the ravani will have absorbed it all.

9. Sprinkle some pistachio nuts on the surface of each individual piece of ravani.

Tip:
Serve with vanilla ice cream. Enjoy!

GREEK SOFT CHRISTMAS HONEY COOKIES
(Μελομακάρονα)

Makes a batch of 30 cookies

In a Greek house, it does not smell like Christmas until these little beauties are made. The sweet smell from these little treats spreads in the house, and the scent of cinnamon fills the nostrils with joy! They are very easy and quick to bake, which is just as well, because they get eaten very quickly. This is a fantastic dish to make with kids— let them drizzle the honey, and they will be very pleased! So, let's get down to it!

Ingredients

4 cups all-purpose flour

2 tsp. baking powder

1 cup olive oil

1 cup canola oil

1½ Tbsp. cognac

1¾ cups sugar

2 tsp. cinnamon

1 tsp. ground cloves

Zest of two oranges

1 tsp. baking soda

¾ cup fresh orange juice

For the syrup

1½ cups granulated sugar

1½ cups water

1½ cups honey (thyme honey would be best)

½ unwaxed lemon, juice and zest

½ cup ground pistachio nuts or walnuts

Method

1. Preheat the oven to 325°F.
2. Sift the flour and the baking powder into a large bowl.
3. In a separate bowl, combine the olive oil, canola oil, cognac, sugar, cinnamon, ground cloves, and the orange zest.

4. Dissolve the baking soda in the orange juice and add it to the mixture. Whisk briskly.

5. Add flour from Step 2 to the wet mixture and ensure it is well blended. Don't overwork the mixture. The resulting dough has to be light and oily.

6. Mold small segments of the dough into little walnut-size oblong pieces.

7. Place on a shallow oven pan. Proceed to score the surface with a fork.

8. Bake for approximately 25 minutes, until golden brown.

9. Set aside to cool.

10. For the syrup, combine the sugar, water, and honey in a pan and boil for 3 minutes after the mix starts bubbling away. Reduce the heat to the lowest setting possible and start dipping the cookies in one by one, in order to absorb some of the syrup. Put on a nice presentation platter and sprinkle with the ground pistachios or walnuts.

Tip:
After dipping the cookies in the syrup, pour the remaining syrup over the biscuits for extra deliciousness.

AUNTIE SOFIA'S SWEET PUMPKIN PIE
(Κολοκυθένια)

Serves 12

Throughout my life, while learning how to cook and later on when I just needed that extra bit of information on ingredients, times, etc., my first port of call was my dear Auntie Sofia. I am so grateful to her for this incredibly scrumptious recipe. She actually remained on the phone while I was preparing this one, just in case I messed up!

Ingredients

2 packets of filo pastry

1 large pumpkin

1 cup olive oil, divided

2 cups of Demerara sugar

1½ cups mixed sultanas and raisins

1½ cups walnuts (coarsely grated)

½ cup of lightly toasted sesame seeds + extra for topping

2 pinches nutmeg

2 Tbsp. ground cinnamon

1 cup butter (melted)

Method

1. Preheat the oven to 350°F.
2. Place 5 filo sheets on a shallow baking tray and bake for approximately 15 minutes.
3. Once golden brown, remove the baked filo pastry sheets and break into little pieces.
4. Cut the pumpkin into chunks and coarsely grate in a food processor, or by using a hand grater.
5. Heat ⅓ cup olive oil in a large pan.

6. Add the grated pumpkin and sauté for approximately 15 minutes, regularly stirring, until the pumpkin's juices have absorbed and it becomes soft. Leave it aside to cool down.

7. Add the filo pastry pieces, sugar, sultanas, raisins, walnuts, sesame seeds, nutmeg, and cinnamon to the pumpkin. Stir well.

8. Layer half the remaining filo pastry sheets in your baking dish, one by one, and brush the melted butter on each one before you layer the next on top.

9. Pour the pumpkin mixture on the pastry sheets.

10. Brush each remaining filo pastry sheet with the melted butter and layer them on top. Tuck the edges in.

11. Score the surface diagonally, sprinkle with sesame seeds, and bake for approximately 45 minutes, until golden brown.

GREEK CHURROS
(Τουλουμπάκια)

Makes a batch of 30

Very similar to the Spanish churros, touloumpakia (pronounced too-loo-ba-kia) are syrupy delight that have their roots in . . . who cares? They are so amazing! I remember once my mum came to my school unannounced and saw me smoking behind the toilet shelter (I know, right, we have all been there). After a very uncomfortable exchange, leading to me turning beet red from embarrassment, we went home. You could cut the atmosphere with a knife, until my mother said, "Come on, I have made touloumpakia." Needless to say, everything was back to normal very fast, with the family exchanging stories about them being caught behind the proverbial smoking shelter by their parents. Food, eh? What a magnificent thing, especially when sugar is involved. It can appease even a Tasmanian devil, I tell you!

Ingredients

¾ cup all-purpose or strong white flour

5 Tbsp. semolina flour

½ cup butter, room temperature

1½ cup sugar

1 Tbsp. vanilla extract

Pinch of salt

1 cup water

4 eggs

Sunflower oil for frying

For the syrup

3 cups sugar

3 cups water

½ cup honey

Zest of one lemon

1 tsp. lemon juice

Method

1. In a mixing bowl mix the flour, semolina, butter, sugar, vanilla extract, salt, and water. Mix thoroughly.
2. Gradually add the eggs and mix at a slow speed setting, until the mixture is homogenized.

3. Knead the dough and leave to rest for approximately 10 minutes.

For the syrup
1. Mix sugar, water, honey, and zest together and bring to the boil, until the syrup thickens slightly. Add the lemon juice just before you take the pan off the heat.

Frying
1. Pour the pastry in a piping bag with an 8B piping nozzle attachment. Squeeze the pastry through until you have approximately a 3 inch piece. Repeat the process until no mixture is left.
2. Heat the oil and fry the touloumpakia until they turn golden brown.
3. Remove from the pan and immediately submerge the touloumpakia in syrup.

Tip:
Dip in melted chocolate for an even more sinful delight!

INDEX

A

Allspice
    Smyrna Meatballs, 52–53
Almonds
    Hard Christmas Cookies, 128–129
Asparagus
    Sea Bream with Vegetables and
        Potatoes, 70
Auntie Sofia's Sweet Pumpkin Pie,
    140–141

B

Basil
    Halloumi Pita with Salad and Black
        Forest Ham, 80–81
    Linguine with Homemade Pesto, 90
Bean Broth, 48–49
Beans
    Butter Beans, 8–9
    Quick and Easy Green Beans, 46
Béchamel sauce, 72, 76
Beef
    Mince Pie, 56–57
    Moussaka, 72–75
    Smyrna Meatballs, 52–53
Beef Stifado, 84–85
Biscotti
    Twice-Baked Greek Style Biscotti,
        134–135
Black Olive Bread, 120–121
Bougatsa, 126–127
Brandy
    Hard Christmas Cookies, 128–129
Bread
    Moussaka, 72–75

    Smyrna Meatballs, 52–53
Bulgur Wheat and Feta Cheese Salad,
    22–23
Butter Beans, 8–9

C

Capers
    Sea Bream with Vegetables and
        Potatoes, 70
Carrot
    Chicken Giouvetsi, 58–59
    Family Pork Roast, 62–63
    Garden Peas with Carrots and
        Potatoes, 30–31
    Mince Pie, 56–57
    Mum's Chicken and Rice Soup with a
        Lemon and Egg Sauce, 50–51
    Puy Lentil Stew, 44
    Quick and Easy Green Beans, 46
    Quick and Easy Leftover Pork and
        Orzo Pasta Stew, 40–41
    Shrimp in a Tomato and Ouzo Sauce,
        20–21
Cayenne
    Harissa Dip, 106
Celery
    Bean Broth, 48–49
    Mince Pie, 56–57
Chard
    Seafood Salad, 16
Cheese
    cream cheese
        Spinach and Feta Cheese Pie,
            34–36
    feta

Black Olive Bread, 120–121

Bulgur Wheat and Feta Cheese
Salad, 22–23

Feta Cheese and Sweet Red
Pepper Dip, 102

Peasant's Salad, 12–13

Shrimp in a Tomato and Ouzo
Sauce, 20–21

Spinach and Feta Cheese Pie,
34–36

Swirly Cheese Pie, 18–19

Traditional Lettuce Salad With a
Vinaigrette Sauce, 10–11

Gouda
Mum's Stuffed Vegetables,
86–87

Gruyère
Mince Pie, 56–57
Moussaka, 72–75

halloumi
Halloumi Pie, 116
Halloumi Pita with Salad and
Black Forest Ham, 80–81

mozzarella
Chicken Giouvetsi, 58–59

parmesan
Linguine with Homemade Pesto,
90

ricotta
Swirly Cheese Pie, 18–19

saganaki
Honey and Sesame Cheese,
14–15

Chestnuts
Bulgur Wheat and Feta Cheese Salad,
22–23

Chicken
Lemon Chicken with Rice, 54–55

Mum's Chicken and Rice Soup with a
Lemon and Egg Sauce, 50–51

Wine and Tomato Chicken with
Linguine, 88–89

Yiota's Chicken Kebab, 60–61

Chicken Breast with Mediterranean
Roasted Vegetables, 78–79

Chicken Giouvetsi, 58–59

Chickpeas
Hummus, 100

Chickpea Soup, 32–33

Chili flakes
Butter Beans, 8–9
Harissa Dip, 106

Chocolate praline
Greek Doughnuts, 132–133

Cinnamon
Auntie Sofia's Sweet Pumpkin Pie,
140–141

Cream-Filled Filo Pastry Pie—
Bougatsa, 126–127

Fried Filo Pastry Bites in Syrup,
130–131

Greek Soft Christmas Honey
Cookies, 138–139

Ravani, 136–137

Smyrna Meatballs, 52–53

Twice-Baked Greek Style Biscotti,
134–135

Cloves
Twice-Baked Greek Style Biscotti,
134–135

Cod
Mama Vivi's Haddock with Leeks,
66–67

Cognac
Greek Soft Christmas Honey
Cookies, 138–139

Cookies
  Greek Soft Christmas Honey
    Cookies, 138–139
  Hard Christmas Cookies, 128–129
Cream-Filled Filo Pastry Pie—Bougatsa,
  126–127
Cucumber
  Halloumi Pita with Salad and Black
    Forest Ham, 80–81
  Peasant's Salad, 12–13
  Traditional Lettuce Salad With a
    Vinaigrette Sauce, 10–11
  Tzatziki, 94
Cumin
  Smyrna Meatballs, 52–53

D
Dill
  Garden Peas with Carrots and
    Potatoes, 30–31
  Shrimp in a Tomato and Ouzo Sauce,
    20–21
  Spinach and Feta Cheese Pie, 34–36
  Stuffed Squid, 37–39
  Tzatziki, 94
  Vine Leaf and Rice Rolls, 6–7
Doughnuts, 132–133
Dutch crispbakes
  Moussaka, 72–75
  Pasta Pie, 76–77

E
Eggplant
  Chicken Breast with Mediterranean
    Roasted Vegetables, 78–79
  Moussaka, 72–75
  Mum's Stuffed Vegetables, 86–87
Eggplant Dip, 96

Eggs
  Moussaka, 72–75
  Mum's Chicken and Rice Soup with a
    Lemon and Egg Sauce, 50–51
  Pasta Pie, 76–77
  Smyrna Meatballs, 52–53
  Swirly Cheese Pie, 18–19

F
Family Pork Roast, 62–63
Fennel seed
  Shrimp in a Tomato and Ouzo Sauce,
    20–21
  Twice-Baked Greek Style Biscotti,
    134–135
Feta Cheese and Sweet Red Pepper Dip,
  102
Filo sheets
  Auntie Sofia's Sweet Pumpkin Pie,
    140–141
  Cream-Filled Filo Pastry Pie—
    Bougatsa, 126–127
  Fried Filo Pastry Bites in Syrup,
    130–131
  Mince Pie, 56–57
  Swirly Cheese Pie, 18–19
Fish
  Mama Vivi's Haddock with Leeks,
    66–67
  Sea Bream with Vegetables and
    Potatoes, 70
  Trout Fillet with Spinach, 68–69
Fried Filo Pastry Bites in Syrup,
  130–131

G
Garden Peas with Carrots and Potatoes,
  30–31

Garlic
  Bean Broth, 48–49
  Bulgur Wheat and Feta Cheese Salad,
    22–23
  Butter Beans, 8–9
  Chicken Breast with Mediterranean
    Roasted Vegetables, 78–79
  Chicken Giouvetsi, 58–59
  Eggplant Dip, 96
  Family Pork Roast, 62–63
  Granddad Gergios's Garlic Potatoes,
    110
  Hummus, 100
  Lemon Chicken with Rice, 54–55
  Linguine with Homemade Pesto, 90
  Mama Vivi's Haddock with Leeks,
    66–67
  Moussaka, 72–75
  Okras Giahni, 82–83
  Pasta Pie, 76–77
  Potato Salad with Greek Yogurt, 26
  Puy Lentil, Tuna, and Rice Salad, 24
  Puy Lentil Stew, 44
  Quick and Easy Green Beans, 46
  Quick and Easy Leftover Pork and
    Orzo Pasta Stew, 40–41
  Shrimp in a Tomato and Ouzo Sauce,
    20–21
  Smyrna Meatballs, 52–53
  Steamed Mussels, 64
  Stuffed Squid, 37–39
  Sweet Red Pepper Salsa Dip, 104
  Trout Fillet with Spinach, 68–69
  Tzatziki, 94
  Wine and Tomato Chicken with
    Linguine, 88–89
Granddad Gergios's Garlic Potatoes, 110
Greek Churros, 142–143

Greek Doughnuts, 132–133
Greek Pita Bread, 114
  Halloumi Pita with Salad and Black
    Forest Ham, 80–81
  Yiota's Chicken Kebab, 60–61
Greek Soft Christmas Honey Cookies,
  138–139
Green beans
  Quick and Easy Green Beans, 46
Green bell pepper
  Mum's Stuffed Vegetables, 86–87
Green onions
  Garden Peas with Carrots and
    Potatoes, 30–31
  Granddad Gergios's Garlic Potatoes,
    110
  Stuffed Squid, 37–39
  Vine Leaf and Rice Rolls, 6–7

H
Haddock
  Mama Vivi's Haddock with Leeks,
    66–67
Halloumi Pie, 116
Halloumi Pita with Salad and Black
  Forest Ham, 80–81
Ham
  Halloumi Pita with Salad and Black
    Forest Ham, 80–81
Hard Christmas Cookies, 128–129
Harissa Dip, 106
Honey
  Family Pork Roast, 62–63
  Greek Churros, 142–143
  Greek Doughnuts, 132–133
  Greek Soft Christmas Honey
    Cookies, 138–139
  Honey and Sesame Cheese, 14–15

Traditional Lettuce Salad With a
    Vinaigrette Sauce, 10–11
Honey and Sesame Cheese, 14–15
Hummus, 100

L
Lagana Bread, 118–119
Leek
    Chicken Giouvetsi, 58–59
    Mama Vivi's Haddock with Leeks,
        66–67
    Shrimp in a Tomato and Ouzo Sauce,
        20–21
Lemon Chicken with Rice, 54–55
Lentils
    Puy Lentil, Tuna, and Rice Salad, 24
    Puy Lentil Stew, 44
Lettuce
    Seafood Salad, 16
    Traditional Lettuce Salad With a
        Vinaigrette Sauce, 10–11
Linguine with Homemade Pesto, 90
Linseed
    Seeded Bread with Sultanas and
        Raisins, 122–123

M
Mama Vivi's Haddock with Leeks, 66–67
Milk
    Pasta Pie, 76–77
Mince Pie, 56–57
Mint
    Bulgur Wheat and Feta Cheese Salad,
        22–23
    Halloumi Pie, 116
    Halloumi Pita with Salad and Black
        Forest Ham, 80–81
    Mum's Stuffed Vegetables, 86–87

Puy Lentil, Tuna, and Rice Salad, 24
    Spinach and Feta Cheese Pie, 34–36
    Vine Leaf and Rice Rolls, 6–7
Mizuna
    Seafood Salad, 16
Moussaka, 72–75
Mum's Chicken and Rice Soup with a
    Lemon and Egg Sauce, 50–51
Mum's Stuffed Vegetables, 86–87
Mushrooms
    Family Pork Roast, 62–63
Mussels
    Seafood Salad, 16
    Steamed Mussels, 64
Mustard
    Traditional Lettuce Salad With a
        Vinaigrette Sauce, 10–11

N
Nutmeg
    Auntie Sofia's Sweet Pumpkin Pie,
        140–141
    Hard Christmas Cookies, 128–129
    Moussaka, 72–75
    Pasta Pie, 76–77

O
Octopus
    Seafood Salad, 16
Okras Giahni, 82–83
Olives
    Black Olive Bread, 120–121
    Chicken Breast with Mediterranean
        Roasted Vegetables, 78–79
    Halloumi Pita with Salad and Black
        Forest Ham, 80–81
    Peasant's Salad, 12–13
    Puy Lentil, Tuna, and Rice Salad, 24

Traditional Lettuce Salad With a
    Vinaigrette Sauce, 10–11
Onion. *See also* Green onions
    Bean Broth, 48–49
    Beef Stifado, 84–85
    Butter Beans, 8–9
    Chicken Breast with Mediterranean
        Roasted Vegetables, 78–79
    Chicken Giouvetsi, 58–59
    Chickpea Soup, 32–33
    Eggplant Dip, 96
    Family Pork Roast, 62–63
    Garden Peas with Carrots and
        Potatoes, 30–31
    Lemon Chicken with Rice, 54–55
    Mama Vivi's Haddock with Leeks,
        66–67
    Mince Pie, 56–57
    Moussaka, 72–75
    Pasta Pie, 76–77
    Peasant's Salad, 12–13
    Potato Salad with Greek Yogurt, 26
    Puy Lentil, Tuna, and Rice Salad,
        24
    Puy Lentil Stew, 44
    Quick and Easy Green Beans, 46
    Quick and Easy Leftover Pork and
        Orzo Pasta Stew, 40–41
    Sea Bream with Vegetables and
        Potatoes, 70
    Shrimp in a Tomato and Ouzo Sauce,
        20–21
    Spinach and Feta Cheese Pie, 34–36
    Steamed Mussels, 64
    Stuffed Squid, 37–39
    Traditional Lettuce Salad With a
        Vinaigrette Sauce, 10–11
    Vine Leaf and Rice Rolls, 6–7

Wine and Tomato Chicken with
    Linguine, 88–89
Yellow Split Pea Dip, 98
Yiota's Chicken Kebab, 60–61
Orange juice
    Greek Soft Christmas Honey Cookies,
        138–139
    Twice-Baked Greek Style Biscotti,
        134–135
Orange peel
    Twice-Baked Greek Style Biscotti,
        134–135
Orange zest
    Greek Soft Christmas Honey Cookies,
        138–139
    Hard Christmas Cookies, 128–129
Oregano
    Beef Stifado, 84–85
    Bulgur Wheat and Feta Cheese Salad,
        22–23
    Chicken Breast with Mediterranean
        Roasted Vegetables, 78–79
    Family Pork Roast, 62–63
    Feta Cheese and Sweet Red Pepper
        Dip, 102
    Lemon Chicken with Rice, 54–55
    Mince Pie, 56–57
    Moussaka, 72–75
    Mum's Stuffed Vegetables, 86–87
    Pasta Pie, 76–77
    Peasant's Salad, 12–13
    Potato Salad with Greek Yogurt, 26
    Quick and Easy Leftover Pork and
        Orzo Pasta Stew, 40–41
    Sea Bream with Vegetables and
        Potatoes, 70
    Sweet Red Pepper Salsa Dip, 104
    Trout Fillet with Spinach, 68–69

Yiota's Chicken Kebab, 60–61
Orzo
    Chicken Giouvetsi, 58–59
    Quick and Easy Leftover Pork and
        Orzo Pasta Stew, 40–41
Ouzo
    Shrimp in a Tomato and Ouzo Sauce,
        20–21
    Stuffed Squid, 37–39

P
Paprika
    Hummus, 100
    Potato Salad with Greek Yogurt, 26
Pasta
    Chicken Giouvetsi, 58–59
    Linguine with Homemade Pesto,
        90
    Quick and Easy Leftover Pork and
        Orzo Pasta Stew, 40–41
    Wine and Tomato Chicken with
        Linguine, 88–89
Pasta Pie, 76–77
Peas
    garden
        Garden Peas with Carrots and
            Potatoes, 30–31
    split
        Yellow Split Pea Dip, 98
Peasant's Salad, 12–13
Pesto
    Linguine with Homemade Pesto, 90
Pine nuts
    Bulgur Wheat and Feta Cheese Salad,
        22–23
    Linguine with Homemade Pesto, 90
    Mum's Stuffed Vegetables, 86–87
    Spinach and Feta Cheese Pie, 34–36

Vine Leaf and Rice Rolls, 6–7
Pistachio nuts
    Greek Soft Christmas Honey
        Cookies, 138–139
    Ravani, 136–137
Pomegranate
    Bulgur Wheat and Feta Cheese Salad,
        22–23
Pork
    Family Pork Roast, 62–63
    Mince Pie, 56–57
    Moussaka, 72–75
    Pasta Pie, 76–77
    Quick and Easy Leftover Pork and
        Orzo Pasta Stew, 40–41
    Smyrna Meatballs, 52–53
Potatoes
    Bean Broth, 48–49
    Family Pork Roast, 62–63
    Garden Peas with Carrots and
        Potatoes, 30–31
    Granddad Gergios's Garlic Potatoes,
        110
    Mama Vivi's Haddock with Leeks,
        66–67
    Moussaka, 72–75
    Mum's Chicken and Rice Soup with a
        Lemon and Egg Sauce, 50–51
    Mum's Stuffed Vegetables, 86–87
    Puy Lentil Stew, 44
    Quick and Easy Green Beans, 46
    Sea Bream with Vegetables and
        Potatoes, 70
    Yiota's Chicken Kebab, 60–61
Potato Salad with Greek Yogurt, 26
Praline
    Greek Doughnuts, 132–133
Pumpkin

Auntie Sofia's Sweet Pumpkin Pie,
140–141
Pumpkins seeds
Seeded Bread with Sultanas and
Raisins, 122–123
Puy Lentil, Tuna, and Rice Salad, 24
Puy Lentil Stew, 44

Q
Quick and Easy Green Beans, 46
Quick and Easy Leftover Pork and Orzo
Pasta Stew, 40–41

R
Raisins
Auntie Sofia's Sweet Pumpkin Pie,
140–141
Mum's Stuffed Vegetables, 86–87
Seeded Bread with Sultanas and
Raisins, 122–123
Twice-Baked Greek Style Biscotti,
134–135
Vine Leaf and Rice Rolls, 6–7
Ravani, 136–137
Red batavia
Seafood Salad, 16
Red bell pepper
Feta Cheese and Sweet Red Pepper
Dip, 102
Harissa Dip, 106
Mum's Chicken and Rice Soup with a
Lemon and Egg Sauce, 50–51
Sweet Red Pepper Salsa Dip, 104
Rice
Lemon Chicken with Rice, 54–55
Mum's Chicken and Rice Soup with a
Lemon and Egg Sauce, 50–51
Mum's Stuffed Vegetables, 86–87

Puy Lentil, Tuna, and Rice Salad, 24
Stuffed Squid, 37–39
Vine Leaf and Rice Rolls, 6–7
Rosemary
Beef Stifado, 84–85
Family Pork Roast, 62–63
Lemon Chicken with Rice, 54–55
Mince Pie, 56–57
Rose water
Hard Christmas Cookies, 128–129

S
Scallions
Potato Salad with Greek Yogurt, 26
Sea Bream with Vegetables and Potatoes,
70
Seafood Salad, 16
Seeded Bread with Sultanas and Raisins,
122–123
Sesame Paste, 108
Sesame seeds
Auntie Sofia's Sweet Pumpkin Pie,
140–141
Black Olive Bread, 120–121
Honey and Sesame Cheese, 14–15
Lagana Bread, 118–119
Seeded Bread with Sultanas and
Raisins, 122–123
Twice-Baked Greek Style Biscotti,
134–135
Shrimp in a Tomato and Ouzo Sauce,
20–21
Smyrna Meatballs, 52–53
Spinach
Seafood Salad, 16
Spinach and Feta Cheese Pie, 34–36
Trout Fillet with Spinach, 68–69
Spinach and Feta Cheese Pie, 34–36

Split peas
    Yellow Split Pea Dip, 98
Squid
    Seafood Salad, 16
    Stuffed Squid, 37–39
Steamed Mussels, 64
Stuffed Squid, 37–39
Sultanas
    Auntie Sofia's Sweet Pumpkin Pie,
        140–141
    Seeded Bread with Sultanas and
        Raisins, 122–123
    Twice-Baked Greek Style Biscotti,
        134–135
Sunflower seeds
    Seeded Bread with Sultanas and
        Raisins, 122–123
Sweet Red Pepper Salsa Dip, 104
Swirly Cheese Pie, 18–19

T
Tahini
    Hummus, 100
    Puy Lentil, Tuna, and Rice Salad, 24
Thyme
    Family Pork Roast, 62–63
    Mince Pie, 56–57
Tomatoes
    Beef Stifado, 84–85
    Butter Beans, 8–9
    Chicken Breast with Mediterranean
        Roasted Vegetables, 78–79
    Chicken Giouvetsi, 58–59
    Halloumi Pita with Salad and Black
        Forest Ham, 80–81
    Mama Vivi's Haddock with Leeks,
        66–67
    Moussaka, 72–75

Mum's Stuffed Vegetables, 86–87
Okras Giahni, 82–83
Peasant's Salad, 12–13
Quick and Easy Green Beans, 46
Quick and Easy Leftover Pork and
    Orzo Pasta Stew, 40–41
Sea Bream with Vegetables and
    Potatoes, 70
Shrimp in a Tomato and Ouzo Sauce,
    20–21
Smyrna Meatballs, 52–53
Stuffed Squid, 37–39
Wine and Tomato Chicken with
    Linguine, 88–89
Yiota's Chicken Kebab, 60–61
Tomato passata
    Beef Stifado, 84–85
    Mum's Stuffed Vegetables, 86–87
Tomato puree
    Bean Broth, 48–49
    Chicken Giouvetsi, 58–59
    Garden Peas with Carrots and
        Potatoes, 30–31
    Mama Vivi's Haddock with Leeks,
        66–67
    Mince Pie, 56–57
    Moussaka, 72–75
    Mum's Stuffed Vegetables, 86–87
    Pasta Pie, 76–77
    Quick and Easy Green Beans, 46
    Shrimp in a Tomato and Ouzo Sauce,
        20–21
    Wine and Tomato Chicken with
        Linguine, 88–89
Traditional Lettuce Salad With a
    Vinaigrette Sauce, 10–11
Trout Fillet with Spinach, 68–69
Tuna

Puy Lentil, Tuna, and Rice Salad, 24
Twice-Baked Greek Style Biscotti,
    134–135
Tzatziki, 94
    Yiota's Chicken Kebab, 60–61

V
Vinegar
    balsamic
        Seafood Salad, 16
        Traditional Lettuce Salad With a
            Vinaigrette Sauce, 10–11
    red wine
        Beef Stifado, 84–85
        Okras Giahni, 82–83
        Puy Lentil Stew, 44
        Smyrna Meatballs, 52–53
    white wine
        Spinach and Feta Cheese Pie,
            34–36
Vine Leaf and Rice Rolls, 6–7

W
Walnuts
    Auntie Sofia's Sweet Pumpkin Pie,
        140–141
    Greek Soft Christmas Honey
        Cookies, 138–139
    Seeded Bread with Sultanas and
        Raisins, 122–123
Wine
    Beef Stifado, 84–85

red
    Smyrna Meatballs, 52–53
    Twice-Baked Greek Style Biscotti,
        134–135
    Wine and Tomato Chicken with
        Linguine, 88–89
white
    Chicken Giouvetsi, 58–59
    Steamed Mussels, 64
    Stuffed Squid, 37–39
Wine and Tomato Chicken with
    Linguine, 88–89

Y
Yellow Split Pea Dip, 98
Yiota's Chicken Kebab, 60–61
Yogurt
    Black Olive Bread, 120–121
    Chicken Breast with Mediterranean
        Roasted Vegetables, 78–79
    Potato Salad with Greek Yogurt, 26
    Spinach and Feta Cheese Pie, 34–36
    Swirly Cheese Pie, 18–19
    Tzatziki, 94

Z
Zucchini
    Chicken Breast with Mediterranean
        Roasted Vegetables, 78–79
    Moussaka, 72–75
    Mum's Stuffed Vegetables, 86–87

CONVERSION CHARTS

METRIC AND IMPERIAL CONVERSIONS
(These conversions are rounded for convenience)

Ingredient	Cups/Tablespoons/Teaspoons	Ounces	Grams/Milliliters
Butter	1 cup = 16 tablespoons = 2 sticks	8 ounces	230 grams
Cheese, shredded	1 cup	4 ounces	110 grams
Cream cheese	1 tablespoon	0.5 ounce	14.5 grams
Cornstarch	1 tablespoon	0.3 ounce	8 grams
Flour, all-purpose	1 cup/1 tablespoon	4.5 ounces/0.3 ounce	125 grams/8 grams
Flour, whole wheat	1 cup	4 ounces	120 grams
Fruit, dried	1 cup	4 ounces	120 grams
Fruits or veggies, chopped	1 cup	5 to 7 ounces	145 to 200 grams
Fruits or veggies, pureed	1 cup	8.5 ounces	245 grams
Honey, maple syrup, or corn syrup	1 tablespoon	.75 ounce	20 grams
Liquids: cream, milk, water, or juice	1 cup	8 fluid ounces	240 milliliters
Oats	1 cup	5.5 ounces	150 grams
Salt	1 teaspoon	0.2 ounce	6 grams
Spices: cinnamon, cloves, ginger, or nutmeg (ground)	1 teaspoon	0.2 ounce	5 milliliters
Sugar, brown, firmly packed	1 cup	7 ounces	200 grams
Sugar, white	1 cup/1 tablespoon	7 ounces/0.5 ounce	200 grams/12.5 grams
Vanilla extract	1 teaspoon	0.2 ounce	4 grams

OVEN TEMPERATURES

Fahrenheit	Celsius	Gas Mark
225°	110°	¼
250°	120°	½
275°	140°	1
300°	150°	2
325°	160°	3
350°	180°	4
375°	190°	5
400°	200°	6
425°	220°	7
450°	230°	8

ACKNOWLEDGMENTS

If you had told me that I was going to be a cookbook author even as recently as a year ago, I would have laughed in your face and called you crazy, even though I have been cooking all my life. The professional path I have chosen to follow has absolutely no relation to cooking—I am an English teacher, and that is all I thought I would ever be. However, life is strange and leads you down paths you don't think you would ever follow.

Even though I share my life with an author, I never thought I would have what it takes to share the stage with him, so to speak; yet he did. So, this acknowledgment section absolutely has to start with me thanking him for his encouragement, for his belief that I am a woman that can achieve anything she puts her mind to, and for his admiration for that. Thank you, Paul, for being a life companion very few can hope to meet in a lifetime. I adore you and always will.

To the reason I cook, my mother, my idol, the woman I will forever admire even though she is no longer with me. A woman who spent a lifetime looking after people who desperately needed her care. She was a nurse matron, and her name still comes up in conversation as the woman who had a heart of gold. To you, Mother, I owe everything I have and everything I am.

To my father, who looked after me when I was very little, and who had the strength of character to change my nappy when his male friends told him "a man shouldn't be doing that." You showed them what a father *should* be doing and you ended up with a feminist daughter. I know you are proud of me and I thank you for being next to me every step of the way to adulthood, after mum passed away.

When I was growing up, my mother was working full-time in the local hospital and my father was an electrician with a crazy schedule also, so upon my return from school I enjoyed preparing dinner, especially when I saw the pleasure it gave to my family. Food is not just about a satisfied stomach, it is about sitting around the table and talking about life, your day, exchanging ideas and plans—food is communication.